in case of emergency press

We are proud to acknowledge the Traditional Owners of country
throughout Australia and to recognise their continuing
connection to land, waters, and culture.
We pay our respects to their Elders.

We support recognition, reconciliation, and reparation.

Justice of the Holy

Phil Copsey

in case of emergency press

https://icoe.com.au

Travancore, Victoria

Australia

Published by in case of emergency press 2025

Copyright © Phil Copsey 2025

ISBN: 978-1-7637749-2-6

Cover design: Steph Babinczky

Acknowledgements

To Steph Babinczky.
Still the most amazing cover designer!

Dedication

To Liz.
Enough said...
until No. 6!

Table of Contents

Chapter 1 1
Chapter 2 3
Chapter 3 5
Chapter 4 7
Chapter 5 10
Chapter 6 13
Chapter 7 16
Chapter 8 19
Chapter 9 22
Chapter 10 25
Chapter 11 27
Chapter 12 30
Chapter 13 33
Chapter 14 35
Chapter 15 39
Chapter 16 42
Chapter 17 46
Chapter 18 49
Chapter 19 52
Chapter 20 55
Chapter 21 59
Chapter 22 62
Chapter 23 66
Chapter 24 69
Chapter 25 72
Chapter 26 75
Chapter 27 78
Chapter 28 80
Chapter 29 85
Chapter 30 87
Chapter 31 90
Chapter 32 93
Chapter 33 95

Chapter 34..99
Chapter 35..102
Chapter 36..105
Chapter 37..108
Chapter 38..111
Chapter 39..115
Chapter 40..118
Chapter 41..120
Chapter 42..123
Chapter 43..126
Chapter 44..128
Chapter 45..132
Chapter 46..135
Chapter 47..138
Chapter 48..140
Chapter 49..143
Chapter 50..146
Chapter 51..150
Chapter 52..155
Chapter 53..158
Chapter 54..161
Chapter 55..163
Chapter 56..167
Chapter 57..170
Chapter 58..172
Chapter 59..175
Chapter 60..177
Chapter 61..181
Chapter 62..186
Chapter 63..190
Chapter 64..193
Chapter 65..195
Chapter 66..199
About the Author 205

Justice of the Holy

Phil Copsey

Chapter 1

"I don't want you going back, Tony," Susie Signorotto said in a loud voice so the person from Police Welfare who was talking to her husband on the phone could hear as plain as day.

Tony Signorotto turned and gave his wife a withering stare across the room before concluding the call.

"It's been over six months now, Susie, and I'm fine. I need to get back in the saddle. I'm a cop and I have to get back to work," an exasperated Signorotto said to his wife with a steely edge to his voice.

The fact that a serious shooting incident involving a Romanian mafia figure had nearly taken Tony's life did not seem to deter the career police officer. He had gone through several operations on his chest and left hip and had been given the all clear to return to work, albeit with ongoing medical checks and physio appointments for the foreseeable future.

"Don't lie to me. Don't think I haven't been in contact with the police doctors and other people about you. I've put up with enough heroics from you and you need to think about me and Grace very carefully," a now furious Susie said referring to their young daughter as she paced up and down the kitchen of their Carlton home.

"Well, according to the quacks and the shrinks, I'm good to go. I can't stay on WorkSafe benefits. I'm a cop. It's in my blood and you know it," a despondent Tony Signorotto replied.

Susie Signorotto snatched Tony's mobile phone out of his hand and hit redial for the number of Police Welfare.

"The only compromise I will make about this is that you are not allowed out of the station under any circumstances. You can hand over the reins to Kate McLaren, your second-in-charge and be king of your mahogany foxhole and deal with the day-to-day shit, or I will take Grace and walk. I'm dead serious about this, Tony. I've had enough of lying awake at night waiting for some fucking Inspector or Superintendent to knock at the door at three in the morning telling me you aren't coming home," Susie said as she began her rant to the unfortunate Police Welfare person that had picked up on her call.

Tony couldn't do anything but stare at the photo of little Grace that was stuck on the fridge.

A compromise was probably the only way to go, he thought. For now!

Chapter 2

"In your own time, six rounds to impact the grey."

The cacophony of sound that reverberated around the underground firing range at the Melbourne Pistol Club in Port Melbourne was almost deafening, even though the five shooters were wearing earmuffs. The six shots that each person punched into their torso-shaped target sent minuscule pieces of cardboard from their respective booths spiralling into the humid air. The whole scenario was over within a minute.

"Holster firearms and wait for your targets to come back to you," the range controller said as he hit the button to bring all the targets back from their position twenty metres down range.

The tall male who had been shooting from the first booth slid his Glock semi-automatic smoothly back into a well-worn army shoulder holster and stood, staring intently while the targets came back with a whirring sound, as the mechanisms they were attached to brought them to a halt just in front of each shooter's booth. He smiled as he counted six holes, perfectly centred. If the shots had been put into a human being, one or more would have ended its life immediately.

A few groans and sighs could be heard from the other booths as the range controller came out of the viewing area at the rear of the gallery and walked slowly to the first booth.

"Nice grouping," he said as he examined the almost perfect positioning of the holes. "But then again, it's nothing new from what I've seen of your shooting since you've been coming here, Jack," he said smiling as he moved to the second booth.

Jack Ziegler only nodded in reply as he removed his shoulder holster and firearm and placed them carefully into a steel container in the storage area, locking it, and then placing the keys in the hands of one of the range controllers. He then walked quietly to the back of the range and out the door.

The head range controller was looking at the target of the man in the fourth booth when the shooter spoke.

"Very quiet guy," he said, indicating Ziegler as he saw him depart. The range controller replied with a slight laugh.

"He's been shooting here for a while now. Hits centre mass every time he shoots. But then again, for his occupation, that shouldn't be unusual."

"What do you mean?" the shooter said.

"Centre mass. You know… mass. The guy's a priest!"

Chapter 3

It had been a hectic year at the Carlton police station since the shooting of Senior Sergeant Tony Signorotto. Everyone had been impacted by that fateful day, and none more so than Senior Sergeant Kate McLaren.

She was the sub-charge of the station and had been doing both her and Signorotto's job over the previous six months while Tony had been recovering. The station was again running smoothly she thought as she walked into the Lygon Street institution of Dom's restaurant alongside Max Tyler, who she had managed to get transferred to Carlton to help with the workload. It was time for coffee, and she was looking forward to seeing her old friend Dom Santino. She had known him for a few years now and she, along with other members from the station, felt right at home in his restaurant. They sat at their usual table at the rear of the restaurant, and Max prepared to order a short black for himself and a cappuccino for Kate.

"G'day Dom, how's it going ?" Max said.

Dom Santino looked up with a smile. "Max. Good to see you back at your old place. Some of us have missed you."

"Kate approached the new Superintendent and told him that we were short-staffed with the boss being off crook, so he took pity on her and, bingo, I'm back. Just don't know for how long though. Tony has only been back on deck a couple of days and he's just finding his way again. He said he saw you the other night here when he and his family came in for dinner."

"He looks as though he is recovering well from his wounds," Dom said quietly.

"It's little steps, really. The shot that bastard put into him certainly did a job on his insides, but it also chewed up a few major nerves and unfortunately his sciatic nerve. Plays up now and then which means that he gets a bit of a limp going sometimes. The Department is not convinced that he is anywhere near ready to return to full duties and it will depend on a lot of shrinks and other types of doctors' reports over quite some time. He is only back for limited hours a day and then it is on a strict basis that the injuries don't play up," Kate said referring to the shot that the now deceased Romanian mafia member, Bogdan Vulpe, had put into Tony six months before in a tense shootout in Carlton.

It was after that when Tony's lovely wife, Susie, said that time was up and that Tony had served the Police Force for long enough. In the end, she had given up but did get a promise from him that he would stick to the station only and not risk himself on the street. Tony had said yes to that but Kate knew Susie might as well have been talking to a brick wall with the stubborn, Italian bred man that was her husband. Susie had threatened him that if she heard one whisper about him doing anything but clerical duties she would, as she said, *sit on the Chief Commissioner's doorstep as quick as a flash!*

"Anyway, what's news at Carlton these days?" Dom continued.

"Well, as you probably heard, that female Superintendent we had went back to the U.K. with her tail between her legs after botching up that fentanyl operation where Tony got shot, and we've had a couple of replacements since, but one went off into private business and the other went off on a sideways gig to the Feds in Canberra a couple of weeks ago. The new appointment is a young guy who is ex-Special Operations Group by the name of James Collins. As long as we can still have our parties and celebrations continue on here at *Dom's*, then everyone at Carlton will be happy. If you can keep your clientele happy, it's a win-win situation," she said with a cheeky wink at Dom.

"Wait till Tony gets back on his feet properly and we will have a welcome back surprise party for him here. Get some of the old Carlton team back together like the good old days," Dom said, smiling at Kate.

"I'll let them know that the wealthy restaurateur will cover the night," Max said with a straight face.

"Typical police. By the way," Dom said with a wink as he walked away from the table after taking their coffee orders, "don't forget to pay before you leave."

Chapter 4

Gardening was the one therapy that Peter Galbraith found relaxed him the most. That, and a bit of backyard landscaping, was what he needed after a long week as Federal Government head of the Department of Veterans' Affairs in Victoria.

His job was a complex one, dealing with Australia's returned military veterans. Some could be quite good to deal with when it came to issues such as PTSD and related matters, but he and his department managers were becoming increasingly aware that the veterans returning from Iraq and Afghanistan were a lot more volatile towards them than any other returned military they had dealt with. There was still a lot of animosity from certain sectors of the public who put them in the same basket as, years before, soldiers who had served in Vietnam—they had returned to their shores only to have buckets of red paint thrown over them. He and his workers could only do so much to help these newer veterans, but somehow, enough never seemed to be enough for them. Their demands were increasing as more and more news coverage about PTSD and trauma became the daily read at breakfast.

These thoughts were running through his head as he started some spade work in the front yard of his house in Munnering Lane in Carlton North. He and his wife had bought the old miner's cottage over a year ago and had been painstakingly restoring it ever since. However, now was the time to start some of the landscaping work in the very small front yard. Galbraith was determined to have a full cottage-style garden ready for summer, and to do that, he had to dig up most of the yard.

There were several of the side-by-side cottages in the lane, and they had got to know their neighbours well. Peter could quite often be digging away in the yard when one of the locals could be found leaning over the fence only a couple of metres from him, chatting away about anything and everything. He and his partner, Lynette, had really been enjoying the move from their unit in Moonee Ponds. As he was digging away a voice spoke from behind him.

"Looks like hard work there, Peter?"

Galbraith was about to reply to the voice while in the back of his mind he found it slightly strange that he didn't recognise it. He looked into the bedroom window directly in front of where he was digging and saw the reflection of a hooded figure holding a raised firearm. A cold chill went through him as he realised that the gun was aimed at him. He immediately flattened himself on the ground as the gun boomed behind him and two bullets smashed the bedroom window into a thousand shards of flying glass. He lay there for what he thought was an eternity, all the while hearing the thumping sounds of a person running away and disappearing into the distance.

Even more frightening than being shot at was the male voice had used Galbraith's first name before letting the shots fly. He raised himself slowly from the loose earth where he had been digging and looked behind him at the empty lane. Crawling over to the fence he looked in both directions as he heard the front door of his house burst open.

"What on earth happened?" his shocked partner, Lynette, asked in a tremulous voice.

"Some lunatic just tried to kill me. If I hadn't ducked I would have had my head blown off," the now shaking Galbraith said, trying to control the emotion in his voice. Looking back at the house, all he could see were the curtains on the front window flapping in the afternoon breeze. The twinkling of smashed glass reflected in the sunlight. Lynette Galbraith stared at the now shattered window as she attempted to hold onto her husband's arm as he raised himself to a standing position.

"Who was it? Did you see anyone?" she asked.

"No, just a male voice I didn't recognise and a person in a hoodie pointing the gun."

"This has got to be something to do with your job. I'm calling the police right now," Lynette Galbraith said as she raced back inside to get her phone.

Peter Galbraith had called the police before to his workplace in La Trobe Street in the city but this was different. The person knew his name and where he lived. This was frighteningly different he realised as he stood in his garden and felt a shiver go up his spine.

Chapter 5

Sergeant Max Tyler peered over the shoulder of the white-clad crime scene member who was examining the shattered front window.

"What I need will be inside, sarge. The shots have just gone straight through from where the offender fired and he never came anywhere near the house, so no prints to find," he said, picking up his steel forensic equipment case and heading to the front door. Max turned to Peter Galbraith.

"I can assure you, Mr. Galbraith, we, along with the Federal Police, will be investigating this very thoroughly."

"This isn't just a local police job then?" Galbraith questioned as they both stood in the front yard of his house.

"Because you're a senior Federal fugure in a sensitive area, we have to get the Feds involved. From the way you have described the incident, I don't think it was a random shooting to be honest."

Max walked towards his patrol car and, after giving instructions to a junior member, he was about to get into the vehicle when the forensic member called him back to the house.

"Struck it lucky, sergeant. It was good that the owner recalled the two shots, because I found two slugs in the doorframe of the master bedroom. Nine-millimetre rounds from a semi-auto of some sort."

"Now the hard part is to find the shooter," Max replied raising his eyebrows.

"True, but these two rounds were virtually on top of each other in the frame. If Galbraith hadn't ducked as soon as he saw the reflection, he would have had two neat holes through the back of his skull, judging by his height and the location of the rounds. Whoever did this had a very steady hand. It could have so easily been an execution-style murder."

"Yeah, that's what worries me about this. It wasn't some punk letting off a couple of drunken rounds. This was totally premeditated. When you finish up here, get us the forensic report as soon as you can so I can sit down with the Feds and our new Superintendent, who apparently started today. Nice intro to his city beat. Starts off with the Feds on one shoulder and the Chief's office on the other. Hope he likes a bit of pressure," Max said, stepping back into his car and picking up his mobile phone before ringing through to Carlton. After a few rings, Tony Signorotto picked up.

"What's the story, Max? Drive-by, random, or something worse?" the Senior Sergeant asked.

"I think it might be a lot worse boss. No drive-by. It was a walk-by with a very cool shooter who I think knew his intended victim. The only reason Galbraith survived is that he didn't recognise the voice when he was called by his first name, so when he looked up and saw the shooter's reflection in one of his windows, he just did a nose dive into the dirt and stayed there while two zingers almost parted his hair for him. Given all the circumstances which I'll tell you about soon, I think you'd better get the new Super and the Feds in for a meeting today if we can. This Peter Galbraith is the head of the Department of Veterans' Affairs here in Victoria. Something tells me this isn't a one-off, but it might have very nearly been one."

"Don't like this at all, Max. I'll get on the phone right away," Tony said as he hung up and dialled the Superintendent's number in town. He had not had the chance to contact the newly appointed officer since just coming back and was tossing up how he would speak to him when the call was picked up almost immediately.

"James Collins here. I presume that's you Kate?" a confident voice said down the line.

Tony Signorotto was taken aback immediately wondering why he would use Kate's name when Collins answered his own question.

"It's okay, Kate. I've just finished putting in the speed dial numbers for my station Senior Sergeants together with their names. You okay with being called Kate on the proviso that you call me James?"

"Er, absolutely boss," Tony stammered, as he gathered his thoughts.

"Tony. You back on deck? Don't want sir, boss, super or anything like that. James will be fine. I'm here to help you lot and after what I've read about your last Superintendent, I can guarantee you there won't be any grandstanding stuff from this end. Now, how can I help you, mate?"

Tony Signorotto relayed all the information he had on the shooting. Collins did not interrupt once. At the end of his spiel, which included asking for a meeting with him and the Feds, Collins replied, "Tony, leave the Feds to me. I was going to ring you anyhow to arrange a coffee to meet you and Kate, so how about I come out this afternoon with the Feds in tow and we sit down and get to work on this? Sound good?"

"Would you prefer us to come in there? You must be pretty busy seeing you've only just started in town."

"Hate sitting around in this office, Tony. I've always been operational, so I like to get out and about. Besides, you are the busy ones at the stations, especially with you just getting back in the chair, and I want to get a feel for what you do and what you have to put up with out there; so, no, I'll come to you. Just have some decent coffee there."

"We only have good coffee here. Force of habit. Only the best *Vittoria* here with my heritage."

"Done a bit of research on you, Tony. You back your troops all the time from what I've read. See you this afternoon," Collins said.

"Thanks, James, looking forward to it," Tony said before hanging up and starting his computer for a search of the Police Human Resources database.

He found the entry he wanted and perused the career to date of his new Superintendent.

Mmm. Action man himself, he thought to himself.

Chapter 6

"I've assured Peter Galbraith that we will get back to him as soon as we can with some sort of plan," Max Tyler said to the people gathered around the table in the conference room of the Carlton Police Station.

Introductions and handshakes had taken place between them all. The Federal Police Inspector, Ethan Barnes, an expert on the guarding and protection of VIPs and other dignitaries had thanked James Collins, Tony Signorotto, Kate McLaren, and Max Tyler for including him in these discussions prior to them all getting down to business.

"At this stage," Collins said, "I must let you all know that I have briefed Detective Inspector Murray Carter from our Major Crime Squad in relation to the happenings of this morning. I have assured him we will keep him posted on any updates. What I do want to do though is tell you that I have also spoken to our Assistant Commissioner for Crime, and he, along with our Federal colleagues, has agreed to keep this in-house. The last thing we want is for the details to get out that some crazy has tried to bump off the person in Victoria who is responsible for the welfare of our returned veterans. If it does get out we may get a copycat attempt. Do we agree?" All heads nodded. "I'll let Sergeant Tyler give us some more details." Max took over.

"We all know most of the details, but what I want to emphasise is the precise nature of the actual attempt. The forensic people took two slugs from inside the house which were basically side by side in the wood panelling. The shooter never just shot once and threw in a second for the heck of it. Galbraith told me that the shots were one right after the other. I say the shooter was cold and calculating. His voice indicated that. I think he knew that he had just missed his target and took off rather than try some clumsy attempt of climbing over Galbraith's front fence and finishing the job."

"Any witnesses to his running away?" Collins asked.

"No. Got the car crew to canvass all the houses in the lane. No one saw or heard anything," Tyler replied.

"Have there been any threats or as such against Galbraith before?" Kate McLaren asked as she turned to look at Ethan Barnes.

"There have been plenty of documented phone threats that have come in from Iraq and Afghanistan vets, but we've always dealt with those as soon as they happened. There are some vets who blame everyone else for their problems. Also, a bit of abuse as staff have left their building in La Trobe Street for lunch or home, but nothing like this, no," the worried Inspector said slowly.

Collins indicated to Barnes, who began to speak.

"Ethan and I agree that, because Max knows Carlton so well, he'll work this case as a seconded Vic Pol member. You okay with that Max? You'll work out of Fed headquarters," Collins said, looking from Max to Tony and back, knowing what the next question would be and who it would come from. Max nodded his head. Turning to Tony Signorotto he continued.

"Tony, you can upgrade one of yours to Sergeant, and I'll make sure that two Senior Constables from Melbourne will come down here for the duration. Do you have an upgrade in mind?"

To get any sort of upgrade and extra members was always a financial and logistical battle with the bean counters in town, so he jumped in quickly. "If that's a given then, yes. Chloe Schaeffer is due for upgrading, so she can take Max's spot. The extra money should go down well with their upcoming matrimonial plans. Two more troops on the ground are always handy. I'll speak to the Senior Sergeant in town and make sure he doesn't try to offload a couple of duds to us."

"Sorted then," Collins said. "Max, you'll be working closely with Ethan here and reporting directly to him. I'll pass on all the info to Tony and Kate here on my surprise drop ins," he said.

Kate McLaren spoke up. "We need that forensic report on the bullets ASAP. Without that we are really chasing our tails. Also

Ethan, if this is a returned vet then I think we'd better get onto Vic Barracks and get them to tell us, not only who has come back from a tour in the last twelve months or so, but of those who have, who are that proficient with sidearms that they could have done this. All agreed?"

"Good thinking, Kate," Collins said. "Now two things. First is that, as I said before, we keep this under wraps and secondly, we meet again but not here. Members will be asking questions about Max going over to the dark side, excuse me Ethan, no offence intended. No talk of this to anyone else. I don't want this character in headlines in the Sun-Herald. Ethan, you okay with your troops doing the twenty-four-seven sit-off on Galbraith and running him into work and back?"

"Our problem, our troops. Just glad to have a local Sergeant doing point on it," Ethan Barnes said, smiling.

"Okay, anyone know a place where we can catch up in plain clothes and talk between ourselves on this? A secure coffee shop would be handy."

"Think I know the ideal location, James. It also has a very discreet person who owns and runs it and serves *Vittoria* coffee!"

"Great. Let's get to work and nail this guy. Our vets and those who look after them need to be looked after themselves. The old *'who guards the guard while the guard guards you'* theory."

They all stood and started heading for the door. Collins turned to Kate and Tony.

"Now that I'm here, you might as well give me the Cook's tour and we'll have a coffee downstairs and a chat about what I can do to help you," he said smiling.

Chapter 7

The man sat in the back pew of the Church of the Uniting Spirit in Palmerston Street, Carlton with shaking hands holding his head. Tears were running through his fingers at the same time as his sobbing voice echoed through the empty nave. The gaunt-looking individual was dressed in ragged clothes and had a straggly beard that matched his dirty, long, greyish hair. A large plastic striped bag, holding what appeared to be all of his possessions, sat to his left.

There were very few other people in the church, but some turned to stare at the stranger whilst others stood up and headed towards the side door quickly because they presumed the man was going to cause a scene or even become violent towards them if they remained. The pastor, who was laying out hymn books in the front row looked up suddenly and called out to the several departing people.

"It's all right, don't leave. I know the man and he's perfectly harmless."

The majority left but one of the few who stayed back walked over to the pastor and spoke.

"Pastor Jack, how do you know him? You've only been here a little over four weeks and I don't think any of the parishioners know him at all."

The Reverend Jack Ziegler turned and put a hand on the shoulder of the enquiring parishioner.

"He's a returned veteran who fought in Iraq and needs all the help we can give him," Ziegler said.

"I don't disagree with you, Pastor, but we can't have people in here who are making the parishioners uncomfortable with their behaviour, can we?" the man replied.

Jack Ziegler's stare become menacing as he answered.

"Some of you people here may not know that I also served in Iraq as a Minister for the Church of the Uniting Spirit, and I can tell you that these men like our friend here deserve our kindness and compassion, and as long as I run this church, he and any other returned veteran will be welcome all day and all night, and to be frank, I don't care if they upset anyone. He has quite a few other mates who I have contacted and who will be coming here for help. If you don't like that, you can find another church to call your own," Ziegler said with an ever-increasing loud and angry voice directly into the parishioner's face, before walking to the dishevelled veteran sitting at the rear of the church.

The elderly parishioner's face went white as he turned to a friend who had been standing nearby and who had heard the exchange between the two men.

"He went from quiet to totally over the top on you within seconds. How strange," the second man said to his white-faced companion. "So aggressive."

"I noticed the Pastor's residence next door has a lot of those striped bags full of clothes and stuff on the doorstep as I passed the house this morning. A couple of odd-looking men also. You don't think he's setting up some sort of halfway house for returned vets, do you?" the man who had received the tongue lashing from Ziegler said back to his companion as Ziegler raised a hand in greeting to the veteran.

"Rick Hawke, welcome to the Church of the Uniting Spirit my friend. We are here to comfort and look after you," he said as he sat down and put an arm around his shoulder.

"How did you track me down? I haven't laid eyes on you since back then," the wary veteran said.

"Found out through a serving chaplain that a lot of the old Regiment have been doing it hard since the fighting in Western Iraq. The Government has treated you terribly over the years since you came home. I came back to serve in the Ministry of Religion and not the Ministry of Defence. I have no time for any of those pen-pushing bureaucrats. My church here has the means of putting a roof over your heads and getting you back into society with those heads held high. What you need is the right person looking after you all."

"What do you mean by looking after *you all*?"

"Do you remember Billy McKay and Ben Waite from back then?"

"Vaguely. I know Waite lost a leg in a IED hit when he went out with some Yanks on patrol in one of those tin-can Hummers. Word is he got hooked on painkillers while he supposedly got better, but how do you get better after that? As for McKay, I haven't heard of him for years. I think we all became drifters."

"Well, I've got hold of them too, and you'll all be staying here at the Parish house for as long as you want. One of the collections each Sunday will keep you all going. I know you all get service pensions, but that's chicken feed these days. These rich Carlton people can afford to house you while I convince Veterans' Affairs to come up with a lot more cash for you three and others down the track. I hate these Government people and I'm going to make them suffer. There are more ways than one to skin a cat," Ziegler said raising his voice once more, causing the remaining churchgoers to turn and look in his direction.

"When do the other two get here?"

"A couple of days before the brothers return, Rick."

"If they both look and feel like me, you'll have your hands full. Mentally I'm shot. I suffer from PTSD badly, and when I hit the booze, you'd better not be in my line of fire. Those days still frighten me badly and I'd say McKay and Waite will be the same. You'd better warn any of your flock who come knocking on your door. We won't be a pretty sight. If they object about their money supporting us, there might be fireworks too."

"This is my parish now. They'll have to fall in line. My parish, my rules."

Chapter 8

"Carlton 307."

"Carlton 307 receiving, VKC."

"Carlton 307, if you could attend in Lygon Street near Argyle Square, please. A report of a disturbance involving some rough sleepers."

"Carlton 307 on the way."

"Carlton 307, number for the job."

"Carlton 307, my mistake. It's Senior Sergeant McLaren 317788. Just out for a shift seeing what the members have to put up with these days," she said with a small laugh.

"Thanks 307. The big fella sitting with his feet up and delegating already?" The experienced D24 operator asked. All those in town knew that Tony was back and were glad that he was okay.

"Don't worry. He'll have the radio glued to his ear listening to this," she said releasing the transmit button and placing the receiver back on its dashboard clip. "Okay, let's see what this is all about," McLaren said to Chloe Schaeffer who was driving the Divisional van. She performed a U-turn and headed to Argyle Square.

Upon arrival minutes later, McLaren could see that the situation had moved to the eastern footpath of Lygon Street where two males were still struggling on the ground as several others trying to pull them apart. McLaren and her partner got out of the van and went straight to the melee.

"Off each other now, you two," McLaren called in a loud voice, causing both men to look up as they rolled apart.

Schaeffer stood in front of the younger looking street kid as he reached down and picked up his skateboard and started screaming and pointing over Schaeffer's shoulder at the dishevelled, bearded male who stood stock still in an old army greatcoat. McLaren stood in front of him and the look she gave the young lad was frightening.

"He's just a fucking warmonger, the dirty prick," street kid yelled. "My generation don't want or need his type. That's why I told him to piss off from around here."

McLaren spoke to the older male. She picked him immediately. It was the steely look in his eyes. She was constantly seeing the same look in her partner, Tom Cole, a returned SAS veteran.

"You're a veteran, aren't you?" she said softly and with what she hoped was a kind smile. The tall, unkempt male looked down at her. Standing at his full height, she estimated him to be over two metres tall and very well built, and even with his dirty looking appearance, she could see a very proud person. When he looked up he spoke directly to the youth who was trying to act as though he wanted to have another fight, but it was obvious that Chloe Schaeffer had no trouble blocking him in his dubious attempt at stepping forward again. He stood there holding onto one arm and alternately trying to stop his obviously broken nose from bleeding.

"Son, get home to your mother. I was just minding my own business when you came at me. I could have done a lot worse to you. Just go away and leave me in peace."

Street boy kept the abuse coming before Chloe Schaeffer suddenly grabbed hold of his arm, spun him around and slammed him face first onto the bonnet of the police car.

"One more foul rant son and you are going in the back of the van, understand?" she said, pushing his right shoulder down as she raised his right arm sending a quick shot of pain through him with the intention of shutting him up. It did. All he could mutter were the words "he started it".

Before McLaren could speak, one of the men who had been trying to break up the struggle stepped forward.

"He's a liar, officer. I saw the whole thing and this little punk here, indicating the spreadeagled youth, just walked up to the other man and starting spewing antiwar crap at him. The man had just been sitting near me outside this restaurant minding his

20

own business reading a paper. He got up to walk away, but then the idiot kid pushed him in the back and told him to fuck off. Worst thing he ever did. That guy, pointing at the veteran with McLaren, turned, and quick as a wink, he had punched him in the face and twisted his arm around so the kid ended up on the ground being sat on. If I'd been the guy I would have done the same. Absolute self-defence." McLaren turned to the veteran.

"What's your name, mate?"

The veteran replied very quietly, "Rick Hawke."

McLaren walked over to the youth who was now standing with Schaefer's arm still holding him.

"How old are you?"

"Nineteen," street boy replied.

McLaren moved the youth back a few steps and spoke very quietly into his ear for a few minutes after which his eyes opened wide and he slowly walked over to Hawke and looked up at him.

"I'm only apologising because if I don't I'll end up getting charged with assaulting you. So that's it," he said as he went to walk off. McLaren stepped up. "Not quite, son. Haven't heard the apology yet."

Street boy looked daggers at McLaren then up at Hawke. "I apologise," he said, before storming off.

The crowd dispersed as McLaren turned to him. "How about a tax payer funded coffee, soldier?"

Hawke looked at McLaren with tears in his eyes as he nodded in appreciation.

Chapter 9

It was only a hundred metres or so along Lygon Street to where McLaren, Schaeffer, and Hawke stopped for a coffee after informing D24 that the job had been seen to, but they were pursuing 'further inquiries.' The D24 operator easily read into the return call that it was coffee time for Carlton 307.

There wasn't any big decision that had to be made about where to grab a coffee, as it was always going to be *Dom's.* McLaren walked into the restaurant with Schaeffer and indicated to Hawke to take a seat. He didn't do as requested by McLaren but hung back from the table and stared furtively around whilst clenching and unclenching his fingers.

"Don't worry," Schaeffer said. "This is like our second home," she said as a young waiter walked over to them.

"I don't think I really fit in here," Hawke said with a quiet but nervous sounding voice as his eyes darted around the tables and the people sitting at them. "I look a bit worse for wear in these old clothes," he said picking at the dirty looking hoodie he was wearing.

"Doesn't worry us a bit," McLaren said. "I'm sure it isn't going to worry the staff here, either."

The waiter stepped up to the members as Hawke slowly took a seat.

"I know what you two have," he winked at both the police members, "but what about you, sir?"

"Ah, just plain black coffee, if that's all right?" Hawke replied.

"Anything to eat?"

Before Hawke could reply, Schaeffer looked up and spoke as she cast her eye over Hawke's thin face.

"Don't know about you, Rick, but I could go a cheese and tomato toastie right now. I'm starving."

Hawke nodded at the waiter in agreement as McLaren held up three fingers for three toasted sandwiches. She had no intention of eating hers, because she could see the ravenous look on Hawke's face. After several minutes of general talk about Carlton and it's surrounds, she decided to probe him for some answers.

"My partner is ex SAS. What about you?" she said, judging that her partner, Tom Cole was about the same age as Hawke.

"I was never SAS. Just a grunt. Lay on my stomach and ate sand for two years," he said, looking from one member to the other. "Nice of you to bring me in here, but I haven't got any money on me till my pension comes through tomorrow, so if you'll excuse me, I'll just ...."

Kate McLaren lent across and put her hand on Hawke's arm. "This is on us, Rick. You're not going hungry today. Where are you shacked up? You don't look as though you're taking a lot of care of yourself, mate," she said waving her hand at his stubbly bearded face and his worn and dirty clothes.

"I get by. I'm a survivor. Been around the traps a bit, but came down here after some religious guy tracked me down. Said he'd look after a few of us at his church near here, but his flock got pretty pissed off with us being given handouts from the collection plate. The other two are still there but I was getting sick of his constant talk about everything being the Government's fault and we should get more than what we do. Left there a couple of days ago and camped up at that Argyle Square place. Lot of rough sleepers up there, so it's okay."

"Not trying to patronise you at all, but do you want me to find some temporary digs?" Kate said.

"Nah. I'll try and sort something. Just don't want to feel as though I owe anybody something. Do appreciate this though," Hawke said pointing at the approaching waiter.

"Rick, you owe nothing. You fought for this country. I know what it's like. My partner still wakes in fright some nights sweating and shaking from nightmares about what he was involved in over there. A coffee and a roof over your head is the least I can do," Kate replied.

Hawke looked at the two officers as he devoured his toasted

sandwich and gulped down the coffee. He had relaxed a little bit and there seemed to be a mutual feeling of respect and understanding between the three. He said nothing at all until he had finished.

"Thanks guys. That did hit the spot, but I'd better be heading off. Don't like to sit too long in the one spot if you know what I mean," he said, standing up to go. As he did, Kate McLaren reached out to him with a business card on which she had scribbled her own mobile number.

"Ring if you want anything. Bed, company, anything. If you want to drop into the station, the door is always open. Coffee's good too," Kate said with a smile.

Hawke looked at the card and then up at Kate. "Thanks. I'll keep this. You never know."

"No, you don't mate. Cheers."

Hawke then slowly walked out the door.

"What did he mean about not wanting to sit in the one spot for too long?" Chloe asked.

"I've heard Tom say that too. These guys are very wary about standing or sitting too long in one place in case they got hit by a sniper's bullet," Kate replied softly as she looked directly at Chloe.

"Wow, that's scary," Chloe replied.

"They never fully relax. I know because I live with it every day, and Tom's got a really good handle on it."

Chapter 10

A week had gone by and Max Tyler had been spending it searching the databases, not only from Victoria Barracks in St. Kilda Road, but also trolling through the records of returned veterans at RSL House in the city.

There had been about one hundred names of service people from these areas that he had red flagged as 'possible interests', and now he was getting to those who had made threats in any substantial or violent way towards any staff, when Ethan Barnes stood over his shoulder and, after looking at the lists, spoke to him.

"Do you think this will narrow down the field at all?" he said.

"The more I go into this, the more complicated it gets. I'm only looking at returned veterans from the last couple of years. That shooting could've been done by some long-lost mate or relative of some vet, or even some member that is still in the Forces. It's like looking for a needle in a haystack."

"Yeah, you're right there. Even with all these names, we are only looking at ex-service personnel who we think held a gun over there on the front line. What about support staff? Cooks, logistics people and the like. All the background staff that keeps the fighters in the field. They are all weapons trained as well," Barnes said with a tired look on his face.

"Then there's those home-grown agitators that never served but just got involved with all the demonstrations and such that have gone on back here since the first troops hit the ground in Afghanistan years ago." Tyler added

"I've been following that lead myself Max with the help of your Security Intelligence Group. They're compiling a list of any known aggressive demonstrators who have attended any of the 'send them home now' rallies from the past few years. They've also gone right through all the Paramilitary nut groups too, but they reckon they are all show and no-go when it comes time to actually doing anything that could land them in gaol. I've also got the Agencies from every other state doing the same thing. The more I think about it though, I think we have to look more closely at the fact that it was almost an execution that had been planned. No radical would be showing up at any rallies and then turning up to basically murder someone. They're all hot heads who just want their five minutes of fame on the nightly news and can then say how dedicated they are to a particular cause. You'd know the 'rent-a-crowd' that kick off at the big protests better than me."

"I've worked heaps of those rallies and you get to know the ones that are passing the buckets around to get so called financial help for their cause. Passers-by just get conned by them. Anything they collect just goes towards money over the Trades Hall bar or the John Curtin hotel. This shooter was cold and calculated and a good shot with a pistol," Max said.

"Let's put ex-military together with crack shot. How does a returned vet keep up his qualifications with a pistol, Max?"

Max Tyler turned towards Ethan Barnes and smiled slowly.

"Of course. Pistol clubs. They wouldn't be current military, because they would do their shooting at military ranges, and there aren't too many of them in Melbourne. Watsonia and Vic Barracks are the only two. Even the part time military have to shoot at those. Ethan, how about you get back to them and I'll start trolling through the pistol ranges around Melbourne. I know that to be a member of one of those you have to go through your complete history before they'll let you in. Kate McLaren will help me out too. She's a crack shot and trains at the Melbourne Pistol Club down at Fisherman's Bend under the Westgate Freeway."

"Let's hope this narrows it down a bit. I have a feeling this nutcase will try and strike again," Barnes said.

Chapter 11

Tony Signorotto walked into the reception area at the Carlton Police station and strode over to the Constable who had his hand in the air waving the Senior Sergeant towards himself.

"What's up? You wanted me?" Signorotto said looking around at the three members who were busy dealing with all sorts of inquiries from several members of the public waiting in the foyer area.

"Yeah, boss. Sorry but there's a guy here who only wants to talk to the Senior Sergeant," the young Constable said, as he covered the mouthpiece of the counter phone with his free hand and nodded in the direction of the rough-looking male who was standing at the rear of the foyer.

"Any indication about what he wants?"

"No. Seems nice enough but only wants to talk to you."

"Okay," Signorotto said as he walked out from behind the inquiry counter and over to the dishevelled man.

"You want to talk to me?" Signorotto said.

Rick Hawke stood with a surprised look on his face before replying.

"You're the Senior Sergeant?" he said, as he flipped over the business card in his hand bearing Kate McLaren's details.

"One of two. Senior Sergeant McLaren is upstairs. Can you show me the card?" Signorotto said holding his hand out for the business card Hawke was holding. Hawke held it out to him and seconds later Signorotto spoke, this time with a smile on his face.

"You've got the ugly one. I'm the boss and Kate is my sub-charge. Can I help you with anything. Name's Tony Signorotto," he said holding his hand in greeting.

Rick Hawke attempted to wipe whatever grime he had on his right hand off on his equally grimy old army greatcoat. Tony took his hand before he could and shook it firmly.

"We don't stand on protocol here, mate. What's your name,

seeing that you know mine now?" Signorotto said with a laugh.

"Rick. Rick Hawke. Senior Sergeant McLaren said to contact her if I needed any help at all. She shouted me a coffee the other day after some kid took a dislike to me in Lygon Street."

Tony had heard about what happened and was glad that Kate had looked after Hawke. Then again, it was no surprise, seeing that Kate's partner, Tom Cole, was a returned veteran also.

"Yeah, I heard about the little dust up. You'd better come upstairs. Kate will want to see you again, I'm sure.

"Don't want to make a fuss or anything. Just need a minute of her time."

"Actually, why don't I get her to meet us in the mess room. It's her coffee time anyway," Tony said as he led the way, at the same time as calling for a passing member to go and get her to come down.

Minutes later, with Rick and Tony seated in the mess room, Kate McLaren walked in and seeing the veteran drinking a coffee she stood by the table and spoke.

"Rick, who made the coffee?"

Hawke turned from one Senior Sergeant to the other with a look of confusion on his face.

"It's okay Rick. She's trying to be funny because it's not often I make the coffee here. She usually makes mine."

"Wonders will never cease," Kate said. "I make it because the mocha java he makes would literally blow your head off. Anyway, besides that, what made you drop in here, Rick?"

"Well, I decided to go back to the church for a while because I want to try and get some kind of job. Don't care what, but if I look as though I'm trying to make a go of it with employment, it will look better telling someone that address rather than giving my address as somewhere on the Carlton streets. I know I need psychological help and the Department of Veterans' Affairs will help me with that, but I have to start helping myself. Also, if I can get some sort of job then I can get away from that raving Pastor down at the church, so what I was hoping to get was some advice as to where to get some employment around here. Nothing big, but just somewhere to start. If you can't help, no problems."

"That's fantastic. The first step is the hardest," Kate said with a huge smile on her face. "I'll certainly ask my partner Tom if he knows of anything, although I don't think you'd be a candidate right now for the security industry, but you never know. He has a lot of contacts. I'll give him a ring later this afternoon."

Tony looked at Rick and spoke.

"Mate, if you are fair dinkum about work, and I'm sure you are, I think we'll be able to put something together for you. Carlton is a hard-working suburb and the people always look out for each other."

"That would be great if you could. Just need to get that first step," Hawke said enthusiastically. "That run-in with the kid just showed me that I have to get off the streets and back into the real world."

"Enjoy your coffee for now, Rick. Kate and I will both work on it. Why don't you give us a couple of days and pop back in again," Tony said.

Chapter 12

Tony Signorotto and Kate McLaren were as good as their word. Two days later when Rick Hawke came back to the station, Tony and Kate sat him down again.

"Rick, you basically said that you were looking for any work at all. Still up for that?" Tony said.

"I'm not getting choosy at all. In the last two days I've been around service stations, op shops, and a few other places, but I don't think anyone wants to trust me with money for some reason," a rather despondent Hawke said in reply.

"How do you feel about washing dishes in a restaurant in Lygon Street?" a slightly hesitant Signorotto said.

"Absolutely. No problems at all. Tell me more."

"Well," Kate took over. " It's actually where you had coffee with me and the other policewoman days ago. The owners are Dom Santino and his wife Maria. They are Carlton institutions and it's the second home to every member that works here at Carlton. Their night dishwasher is a backpacker and he is moving on with his travelling. Tony and Dom go way back and we just happened to mention we had a veteran who was looking to kick start his life again and he was only too happy to give you a go. You don't mind doing the five to eleven slot, six nights a week? Monday is the slack day so Maria rolls up her sleeves and mucks in."

"Not a worry. When do I start?" an elated Hawke said straight away.

"There's a couple of added incentives if you like it, " Tony said. "If you work out, and I can't see why you wouldn't, you get a feed every day and if you are interested, Dom might let you stay upstairs. He has a pretty nice bedroom and shower up there that he has let the backpacker have really cheap." Tony said.

"So, he'd just take money out of my pay? It's just that I can't pay too much. I'm on a Vet's pension but it isn't anything too flash I'm afraid."

"When we mentioned that you were a returned Vet with a few issues, he dropped the price right down," Kate said, smiling as she spoke. "In actual fact, he dropped it to zero dollars. Something about him being grateful for you serving your country."

Rick Hawke didn't reply but sat still as tears formed in his eyes. Kate McLaren thought she saw Tony's eyes look a bit glazed also but she didn't dare say anything.

After shuffling his feet back and forth beneath the mess room table, Hawke spoke.

"You wouldn't believe how grateful I am. I certainly want the job but I have to get away from other veterans too. It's like being in a constant state of depression being around them. Their problems have to be everyone's problems according to them. A permanent state of doom and gloom. And then there is that bloody priest or whatever. Does my head in. Just angry with the status quo all the time."

"Is he getting on your nerves?" Tony said.

"What pisses me off about him is that he is classified as a returned veteran also. He served over there at the same time as me and the other two, but he acts like he was on the front line with us. The nearest thing he would have come to a tooled-up Taliban would be if he saw one on the television from the mess tent. Just constantly going on and on about what the government owes us. He's only been there a short time and he has most of the parishioners offside, what with trying to look after us, who he calls *his flock*. I won't take anything from him but the other two will. I must be the only one of the three that has finally decided to try and get their act together."

"Sounds like a no-win situation all around," a concerned sounding Kate McLaren said looking from Hawke to Signorotto. She knew only too well about mood swings of returned veterans. Her partner Tom Cole had done two tours of Afghanistan and while he was away, his then wife had been killed back in Melbourne by a hit run drunk driver while she shopped with her little daughter, Summer. Kate first met Tom at a pistol range where he took his anger out on paper targets. They had been together a year or so now and Kate knew that even something like a dropped saucepan clanging on the kitchen floor would have him ducking for cover and breaking out into a sweat in their house. She knew all about depression and anxiety. Tom was much better now and held down a very good management job with a security company. Because of what they had been through together, she would go to great lengths to help out Rick Hawke.

"I'd really like to get out from under that guy. It's starting to feel like living in a compound with him as the religious leader."

"I've only just got back to work after a bit of a mishap months ago, so I have been leaving most things up to Kate here, so if it's all right with her we could go down now to Dom's and you can meet him, if you'd like?" Tony said looking sideways at Kate.

"You aren't going out anywhere, Tony, and it wasn't just a 'bit of a mishap." You know the rules about the return-to-work program that you're on, so don't even think about it. I'll take him down to Dom's," a frustrated sounding Kate McLaren said.

"I'll start washing dishes tonight if your friend likes," an eager Hawke said, wondering at the same time about what Kate said regarding Tony's mishap.

Tony Signorotto stood and spoke as he walked to the mess room door quickly.

"Okay. I'll get you the car keys and you can go with Kate. For reasons that I won't go into, I am desk-bound for a while apparently."

Chapter 13

Jack Ziegler knew it was time to take things up a notch or two. There had been no publicity about the shooting weeks before in Carlton. He didn't know if it was because he had missed with his attempted hit on Peter Galbraith, or because Galbraith was a big cog in the Federal Government wheel and Canberra didn't want publicity. Well, it was time to change that.

He hated the abandonment of many returned veterans by the Government and the pathetic way some people played soldier at home but didn't have any idea what the real troops had gone through in Afghanistan or Iraq and the lack of care shown to them on their return home. He had seen what soldiers went through in war, not only in a physical sense but also in a mental sense. He had been proud to be a '*Sky Pilot*' to many of his flock, as he referred to them, in overseas deployment whilst he served with the Royal Australian Army Chaplains Department. He had come back affected as well, but thought that a continuing service to his church would get him through the tough times on return, but the injustice of how he thought his *flock* was treated when they were discharged started to burn a hole through him, and his thoughts started to turn towards violence after he had approached Veterans' Affairs on behalf of some former soldiers and had, according to himself, been shunned and ignored. He now firmly believed that he had to keep playing the *Sky Pilot* and if he had to sacrifice himself for the greater good, then so be it. He wasn't married and had no ties except to the church. He reasoned that he was acting on behalf of God now in his crusade for recognition, so the attempted murder of Peter Galbraith only upset him because he had missed.

Ziegler had walked past the Melbourne University Regiment in Grattan Street many times since the Galbraith attempt. On this occasion though, he had stood across the road one evening and watched as the clean and lean looking uniformed young men and women had walked into the building with a sense of purpose. Poor misguided fools, he thought to himself as he stared at them and up at Regiment's crest. It was symbolised by the Nike, the winged Goddess of Victory and surrounded by an inscription which read *Postera Crescam Laude*, which translated to "*I shall grow in the esteem of future generations*". Ziegler had lost faith in all things military with their penchant for righteousness and violence without accountability.

After observations over several days and nights, together with some inquiring phone calls, he had found that the Commanding Officer of the Regiment was Colonel Simon Forbes. Once Ziegler had his details, it had been relatively easy to pick him out with his khaki uniform and his strutting, overweight manner as he walked from his late model Range Rover into the Regimental building.

Ziegler had a plan in mind for Forbes and if it came off, then without doubt some of the crusty old fools who sat around admiring memorabilia in Returned Services League clubs around Melbourne, believing that God was on their side, would suddenly start spilling their Gin and Tonics and sit up with very wide eyes.

The *Sky Pilot* was about to spread his wings. Firstly though, there would have to be a little wake-up call in Grattan Street to snap the apathy.

Chapter 14

Tony Signorotto had already given Dom Santino a 'heads up' concerning Rick Hawke. Suffice to say that Dom was more than willing to give Hawke a try for two reasons. Firstly, he had been recommended by Tony, whose word Dom trusted more than anybody else he knew, and secondly, from a practical point of view. He had no one else to try as the new kitchen hand and he was losing his present one that day.

Kate leant against the kitchen door as she watched Rick being put through his paces with the industrial dishwashing machine by the outgoing employee.

"Thanks for the offer of the upstairs room, Dom. He won't let you down, and I think he could be a very good deterrent to any would-be burglars too," she said with a laugh.

"First question, though my friend," Dom Santino said. "Can you tell me why Tony isn't down here haggling with me? I know he's come back to the station, but a little birdy told me he isn't on the street anymore. Is that right?"

While Rick was busy looking around his new work place, Kate McLaren told Dom Santino all she knew about the shooting months ago and the subsequent effect it had had on Tony and his family. She knew from talking to Susie Signorotto that she wanted him right out of *The Job* and working where his injuries could be managed responsibly.

"I can tell you Dom, because you know him better than anyone, that it has been hard running the station without him, but I would rather keep doing that than having him come back to work trying to prove himself. He doesn't have anything to prove in my book. The Department won't have him doing anything but administration work from now on, and if he doesn't like it then bad luck. If Susie gets one whiff of him going out in a car for anything, including just coming here, then there will be fireworks. He's going to feel as though he's been basically handcuffed to the station, but there is so much he can pass on to new members, especially the sergeants."

"You probably know that I offered him a partnership in this restaurant just to get him out of the Force. I actually think he was considering it until that shooting, then everything got turned upside down. Maria and I have been regular visitors to his house to see how he has been recovering and, yes, we have felt a bit of tension there whenever he mentioned coming back. Susie has told Maria that she has thought about leaving him and taking their little daughter if he doesn't toe the line. I think we will have to work together and keep an eye on him."

"I've got one of those pig-headed characters at home also," Kate said to Dom in reference to her partner, Tom Cole. "What with him thinking he'll be thirty forever and adding in Tony, we'll have our work cut out, mate."

As she finished speaking, Rick Hawke came from the kitchen into the restaurant with a big smile on his face.

"What's got you looking so happy?" Kate said.

Rick looked at both Kate and Dom before he spoke.

"I know this is just washing dishes and kitchen work, but I don't think you have any idea how glad it feels to be around people and working again. I'd love to have the job if that's okay with you, sir?"

Dom looked over Rick's shoulder to where the regular dishwasher was standing and gave him a questioning look that would be a yes or no to Rick's employment. The man raised both thumbs upwards and nodded his head vigorously. That was good enough for Dom.

"Job's yours then. You can start tomorrow if you want, and you can have the room upstairs. If you are a returned vet who has been given the tick of approval by Tony and Kate, then I'm glad to have you aboard. Another thing though, it's Dom, not sir."

"Fantastic. Just need to…" Hawke said as he looked at the person walking in to the restaurant.

Kate turned and saw the man stop and look back at Hawke.

"What's the matter, Rick. You know him?"

"Yeah, I know him. Just someone who I hope I can get out of my life," he said as he walked towards the person before stopping in front of him and speaking.

"What do you want, Jack?" Hawke said to the Reverend Jack Ziegler.

"Nothing Rick. Just happened to be coming in for a coffee. I should ask what you are doing here? You don't seem to be around the church much anymore. I think you should support your fellow veterans and stick close, don't you?" Ziegler said staring at Jack.

"Jack, I won't be coming back to your church. I like the others, but everyone was becoming dependent on what you said you were going to do for us, but all I see is a couple of ex-grunts that are hanging off your every word, and it also seems to be upsetting your regular churchgoers with us there. I am going my way and in fact I have just been given a job here, so no offence Jack, but as I said, I won't be back."

Ziegler stepped up to Rick's face and spoke slowly at the same time as taking a firm grip on the returned veteran's arm. Rick shrugged it off immediately, which made Kate McLaren step towards the two before Rick turned to her and shook his head. Kate stopped in her tracks.

"You're one of us, Rick. Always remember that. You won't survive without my support. I am doing things to get you your rightful dues from the Government. We have to stay together just like overseas."

"Just go, Jack. I don't need you or your church. I am now becoming independent," Hawke said to a furious looking Ziegler, who turned away and took a couple of steps before turning back and shouting as he pointed at Hawke.

"You need my fellow soldiers. Never forget that."

Ziegler stormed out of Dom's restaurant.

"What was that all about?" Kate said as she and Dom approached Rick.

Rick Hawke proceed to tell both of them his circumstances

since he had arrived in Carlton and the growing concern about the hold that Ziegler was trying to exert over him and the other veterans.

"Sounds like a Sky Pilot that is about to crash and burn," Kate said slowly as she noted a few facts in the folder she was carrying. She underlined the words that Ziegler had said in relation to *'my soldiers'*.

Might have a chat to Max and his team at the Feds about this boy, she thought.

Chapter 15

Billy McKay was getting desperate.

It wasn't that he was ungrateful for the help that Ziegler was giving him and Ben Waite, it was just that he was starting to feel that Ziegler was trying to keep both of them under some form of control.

Ziegler had said that he would try and get them back on their feet by looking out for jobs, but so far, any time they had mentioned this to him, he just waved them away and gave them another small hand-out of money, which both he and Waite had seen coming out of the parish collection boxes. McKay was in between a rock and a hard place. He had to put up with parish under the pew handouts, which he didn't like, but had to take because he had a heroin habit which had kicked off on his tour of Iraq and had never left him. It had really become a raging itch he had to keep scratching and the money that Ziegler was drip feeding them was not getting him far enough with the dealers up around Melbourne University. In fact, he was now in debt to some of them. He didn't mind working the debts off, but so far Ziegler had not come up with anything. The soldier in him told him not to do what he had planned, but the addict in him told him to do whatever it took to feed his habit.

He waited till the Pastor had left the church to go on one of his walks then he snuck into Ziegler's office and started to ransack every nook and cranny in search of items that he could take to the Maxi-Cash Pawn shop in Swanston Street. His plan was to try to get on top of his cash problem and then not return to the church. Even with his habit, he just had a feeling there was something strange about the returned Sky Pilot.

He took his time doing a thorough search of Ziegler's office and had come up with some church property such as candlesticks and chalices, but he knew he wouldn't be able to pawn those without being asked a lot of questions. On the verge of giving up, he looked up at the shelf above an old antique desk and quickly realised there was something strange and out of place. There were a lot of books on religion and the like which appeared to be very well thumbed through, but the extremely large and thick copy of '*The New Testament of Our Lord and Saviour Jesus Christ*' stood looking untouched in its heavy slide-in cover. On the shelf that it sat on there was a lot of dust in front of the other old books, but none in front of the big one. McKay reached up and pulled the large edition towards him. As it came off the shelf he had to grab it with both hands due to its weight. He sat it upright on the desk and slid the cover off it. As the book revealed itself he placed it on the desk and opened it. He stared at the contents. Inside the completely cut out book nestled a well-oiled nine-millimetre semi-automatic pistol. Also sitting comfortably alongside the pistol were two full fifteen round magazines. The package gleamed at him as various scenarios of why Ziegler had this firearm hidden away bounced around in his mind. After quickly placing the book back into its cover and then sliding it onto the overhead shelf he returned to the room he shared with Waite. This was all getting weirder by the day.

Firstly, Zeigler had found himself, Waite, and Hawke supposedly through a serving Chaplain, and then invited them all to come to his church in Carlton where he said he would look after them and find them jobs. It had been a few weeks now and Hawke had gone and there had been no talk of employment. All there had been was Ziegler ranting and raving to anyone that wanted to listen about the corrupt Federal government and the way it treated veterans. It was obvious that some of his parishioners were getting fed up with him and his moods. Money from church collections was going down, because one of the parishioners had seen Ziegler handing cash to the three veterans. McKay had listened to one of his sermons and was gobsmacked with the way Ziegler denounced just about everything. The number of people attending his services had dwindled remarkably, but when questioned about his sermons and persona in general, he totally ignored everyone. He had stated that the church was his and he would run it anyway he wanted.

McKay looked up to see Ben Waite entering the room. He called him over to the corner and proceeded to tell him about the firearm find.

"Don't you think things around here are getting a bit strange, Ben? Don't know about you, but I want out."

"Strange is right," Waite said. He called me into the kitchen yesterday and told me he wanted to make me his second-in-charge. When I asked him what he was on about he said he was trying to locate more returned vets through another of his Sky Pilot mates. Reckons he wants to set this up as a military type of religious base with us vets running it. Sounds like some sort of Jonestown or something to me."

"We need an exit plan from here. Need to get some cash together. Rick got out. Ziegler says he is washing dishes in Lygon Street somewhere. Reckons he has abandoned us. I'm going to ring him and see if he can help us. In the meantime we treat this guy like a ticking time bomb, mate," Billy McKay said to the nodding head of Ben Waite.

Chapter 16

Jack Zeigler tossed and turned as he tried to get to sleep in the small room in the Church of the Uniting Spirit but could not get the thought out of his head that there had been no publicity whatsoever about his attempted hit on Peter Galbraith. He could only conclude that someone was trying to hush it all up. After all, Galbraith was a big public service figure, and if Ziegler had been successful then it would have sent a wave of panic through the Federal Government. Well, if at first you don't succeed then try again. A warm up first, he thought.

Giving up on sleep, he quietly dressed in black jeans, black hoodie, and black sneakers, after which he padded into his office, took down *The New Testament of Our Lord and Saviour Jesus Christ* from the shelf and removed the black Smith and Wesson pistol together with one full magazine containing fifteen rounds. It was time to go to work.

Exiting via the side door, he did not see the figure of Billy McKay crouched in the darkness. He therefore didn't see Billy watching him as he slid the pistol into the waistband of his jeans and then cover it up by pulling the dark hoodie down over it. Ziegler stepped into the darkness. Billy went and woke Ben Waite straight away, telling him what he had witnessed.

"What do you reckon we should do, Ben?" Billy said with a note of panic in his voice.

"I'm doing nothing, mate. How the hell can I with one leg? No good me trying to follow him. Why don't you?" Waite said as he lay back in the small bed that Ziegler had supplied for him in a back room. Billy just rubbed his hands together and hopped from one foot to another.

"I dunno," Billy said as the sweat poured down his face. "He's nuts walking around with a piece on him. Cops will nab him for sure."

Waite looked McKay up and down before speaking.

"You're back on the shit again, aren't you, Billy? I can tell from your moods and the night sweats you get. You're no good to anyone like that and I bet Ziegler knows it. You try and follow him if you like but leave me out of it."

McKay looked at Waite and then suddenly started walking towards the door.

"He's probably too far away now, but I'm going to have a look," he said with his back toward Waite as he disappeared from the room.

Billy McKay's mind might have been affected by the drugs he took but he knew he had to find a way to keep paying for his ongoing supply. Trying to grab some stuff from the church or even doing some thefts from cars wasn't going to be enough to satisfy his thirst. He knew however that there was one thing that would be worth a lot of money if he could get it to the people who wanted it the most. Simple answer was the pistol that he had seen Jack Zeigler tuck into the waistband of his trousers!

McKay ran as quietly as he could out into the street and couldn't believe his luck when, only about fifty metres away he saw Ziegler walk under a street lamp and head away from him. The thought process of how he was going to get the pistol was slowly taking shape in his fogged mind. It would be better to get the pistol here rather than wait and take it out from the bible where he saw it, if indeed it was the same firearm. If he took it from the church, Ziegler would know straight away that it was either himself or Waite that took it and that would mean trouble. If he could somehow get it off him outside the church then it would look like a robbery of sorts.

At three in the morning there was no-one else on the street but himself and Ziegler. He looked around as he followed the pastor and as he passed a building site he saw a short piece of thick off-cut electrical cabling lying near the front boundary of the property. It was as thick as his wrist and about fifty centimetres in length. He reached under the fence and , keeping one eye on Ziegler, he managed to drag the weapon out from under the cyclone wire fence. He looked down at it whilst weighing it up in his hands. Perfect, he thought to himself as he turned around to keep following Ziegler.

Minutes later as he hid behind a car in Grattan Street, he watched Zeigler pull out the pistol and fire round after round into the windows and façade of the Melbourne University Regiment. He couldn't believe what he was seeing and was still in a state of shock when he realised that he was standing in full view of Ziegler who was now running back toward him.

Suddenly they came face to face. The returned army pastor and the returned army veteran. Ziegler grabbed McKay by the jacket and pulled and dragged him down a dirty alleyway running off Grattan Street.

"What did you see, Billy?" a ranting Ziegler screamed at him as he shoved him against a filthy brick wall at the same time as jamming the pistol up to the side of Billy's head.

"Nothing Jack. Nothing. None of my business," a gasping McKay said in reply.

"I'm just evening things up for guys like you and Ben. Don't you understand?" Ziegler said as he pressed the barrel of the Smith and Wesson even harder into Billy's temple.

"I don't know what you're talking about," a now crying and terrified Billy McKay said as he grabbed the barrel away from himself and tried to turn it towards Ziegler.

Both men struggled for control of the weapon but Billy was now almost in a catatonic stupor with fear and the effect of the drugs in his system.

"Billy, let go. I don't want to hurt you; I just didn't know you were watching me. I'm just trying to make things right. Things that this fucking government hasn't done for you guys. I'm on a mission for us. You have to understand. I've got God's work to do. Let go of the gun."

Billy McKay didn't understand Ziegler but he slackened his grip on the pistol just slightly.

Jack Ziegler whipped the gun free, pulled Billy's head back, jammed the pistol under the sweating veteran's chin and fired a round right through his brain. McKay was dead long before he hit the ground.

"God's work, Billy. God's work. Rest in peace, brother," he said as he ran back towards his church leaving the veteran's body lying in an ever-widening pool of blood.

Chapter 17

The shrill sound of the mobile phone ringing next to their bed at four in the morning woke both Max Tyler and his partner Chloe Schaeffer. Bleary eyed, Tyler reached for the device and as he hit the connect button, a voice spoke before he could say hello.

"Sergeant Tyler?"

"Yes," a slow sounding Max Tyler said as the fog of sleep began to clear.

"Sergeant Caldwell here from D24. We have instructions to ring you wherever or whenever there is an incident regarding a military establishment. Looks like we have a complicated one for you. Ready for the details?"

Max Tyler rolled over the still half-asleep form of Chloe Schaeffer and quickly grabbed a piece of paper and a pen from the side table as he put his mobile phone onto speaker mode.

"Shoot," Tyler said.

"Well, that's the second half of the message in fact," Caldwell said with a hint of irony in his voice. "The first bit is that the Melbourne University Regiment building in Grattan Street has been shot up about an hour ago. External damage only. Reported by a passing taxi driver who said he heard shots as he was passing. All he saw was a shadow crossing the road. We have already contacted Inspector Barnes from the Federal Police and he said he would see you there along with Detective Inspector Murray Carter from Major Crimes and the on-call team from Homicide."

"Homicide?" Tyler questioned but quickly realised he had only been told one half of the message.

"Yep. A couple of hundred metres down Grattan Street, we have a male body that, at this stage, appears to have suffered a fatal bullet wound to the head. Anyone else you'd like me to inform?"

"Yeah, you'd better wake up Superintendent James Collins

and see he if wants to join the party. Also, can you get a station car to pick me up?"

"No problem. I'll dispatch one right now. That all? OIC Carlton need to know?"

"No, not at this stage. I can fill him in later this morning," Max thought, realising that Tony Signorotto was on a strict return-to work policy and was totally off the road as far as the Department was concerned. *Won't be happy, but that's not my concern.*

Max dressed quickly and told the half-awake Chloe to go back to sleep knowing that she was on a seven shift in the morning. He walked, still a bit bleary-eyed, out to the footpath and waited a few minutes until he saw one of the uniform cars driving down his street. Climbing into the back seat he was grateful for the takeaway coffee that was handed to him from the member in the front passenger seat.

"Was for me, but you look as though this will be your breakfast as well, sarge," the smiling member said.

"Thanks mate. Appreciated," Max said taking a large gulp of the caffeine.

As the police car was pulling up at the cordoned-off crime scene, Max saw James Collins already standing to one side talking to one of the uniformed night shift members. Before he could even say a word, Collins pulled him aside and spoke.

"I think this could have a connection to the attempt on Peter Galbraith's life, Max."

"The fact that it's a military building?" Max replied.

"That and the fact that the deceased is not only wearing an old military coat and very worn combat boots, but also a set of dog tags. Name on them is a Billy McKay. I'd say a definite vet. Won't put my house on it, but I'm dead sure I'm right."

"I'll talk to Ethan Barnes. He'll have quicker access via Victoria Barracks and should be able to track the name down."

"The Homicide boys will do all the heavy lifting on this one, so you might want to get over to them at the body. Because it had a military tone to it, I've got Detective Inspector Murray Carter on it. One lucky piece of info is that the shooter left a shell casing here and I would say it's definitely from a nine-mill pistol. Liaise with Murray about the results from the autopsy, but I can guarantee you that the Coroner's Court will be doing it later today. This has a nasty ring to it and those up above us are still reeling over the attempted hit on Peter Galbraith. The dead guy doesn't look like he was worth much, but he is going to get VIP treatment. Hopefully by the time the bullet is dug out of him you will have some details about who he was."

Max Tyler thanked Collins and walked over to where the body lay.

Wrong place and wrong time or something else? Max thought to himself looking down at the deceased. He took some quick photos of the body and surrounds and then walked up towards the Melbourne University Regiment building and studied the damage that had been done.

All too coincidental for my liking, Max said quietly to himself

Chapter 18

Tony Signorotto was not a happy man minutes after walking into the Carlton police station later that morning only to be surrounded by members of the Homicide squad together with Superintendent James Collins and Ethan Barnes from the Federal police.

He knew he shouldn't do it, but his Italian blood was beginning to boil at the discussions that were going on around him without him being involved in any of it. Ten minutes of these in-house conversations was enough. He snapped as he turned towards Max Tyler and spoke with venom in his voice.

"As the Senior Sergeant in charge of this station, I can tell you Max, that I am pissed off at all this. Tell me what is going on here and tell me now before I get myself sacked by giving Collins an earful."

Max was not going to tell him what he wanted to know. Not because he didn't want to tell him, but because he respected Tony too much. He needed the full story to come from the horse's head, not the horse's arse.

"Sorry, boss. Give me two secs," he said walking over to James Collins who was in a deep conversation with Ethan Barnes.

"Sorry to interrupt sir, but I think Senior Sergeant Signorotto is about to explode. He knows he isn't allowed out on the road at the moment, but he is feeling as though he is being kept in the dark about all this. He doesn't know about the shooting this morning and after all, he is the OIC of the station. Just saying, sir," a quiet Tyler said.

"You're right, Max," Collins said as he indicated to Barnes to follow him over to Signorotto who was standing in the corridor with a face that looked as though it had been set in concrete. Collins held up both his hands in mock surrender to the Senior Sergeant.

"Tony, my apologies. This is your patch and I should have

known you would be in early. Let's clear the mess room and all sit down. In a nutshell, we've had an early morning murder on your patch and it could be connected with the attempted hit on Peter Galbraith in a way."

"What time of the morning and where?" Signorotto spat back.

"All we know it was early this morning and up at Grattan street," Collins said.

"What's the connection to Galbraith?"

"It was just near the Melbourne University Regiment building which was found to be shot up a bit on the outside. Looks like a handgun used on this guy and there were several casings found outside the building too."

"Okay, let's grab a coffee," Signorotto said as he led the way to the mess room.

Upon entering there were a couple of crews that were finishing and starting who were just sitting down themselves to a coffee.

"All right guys, everyone out. We want this room to ourselves," he said reaching for his wallet and dragging out a fifty dollar note. "My shout if you like up at the Deli of Delights for breakfast. Now all of you piss off," he said with a grin on his face. "If fifty isn't enough to fill your faces, then bad luck."

One of the members grabbed the note off the table and they headed off.

"Love your work, boss," a member shouted back over his shoulder.

James Collins could not have been more impressed with the rapport between Tony and the departing members.

When they had all sat with a coffee and the door had been shut with strict instructions to the morning shift sergeant to keep it that way, Tony spoke.

"Gents, this is my station and, stuck behind a desk or not, I run it, and any information or jobs or such that happen in the suburb of Carlton, I demand to know about them all and be kept updated. My apologies, Superintendent Collins but that's the rule here. All my sergeants, except Max here, who had obviously had a bit of a brain fade, know that. It's stuck in concrete. Now I know all about the Galbraith situation but I want word for word about this morning. Nothing to be left out, okay?"

The look that passed between Collins, Barnes, Tyler and the Homicide members left no doubt in their minds about the capabilities of Tony Signorotto, stuck behind a desk or not.

The next thirty minutes was spent dissecting everything they knew about the killing and the possible connection to the Galbraith situation.

"You said the body had dog tags, Max?" Tony said.

"Yep. Name of Billy McKay. Possible returned vet and by the looks of his clothes, a bit of a rough sleeper. Inpector Barnes is getting onto Vic Barracks this morning and do some digging."

"Yeah, do that, but in the meantime there's a chance I might be able to shortcut you. I'll get Kate McLaren to bring in a returned vet we are helping out at the moment up at Dom Santino's."

"Great," Max said looking around the mess room table.

"Well, if that's all gents, we might as well get back to connecting the dots on this," Collins said as he stood. The other members slowly dispersed as Collins approached Signorotto.

"Welfare Department's choice to keep you inside, Tony, not mine," he said.

"I know that sir. I'll do what I'm told," Tony said with his fingers crossed on both hands behind his back and with a slight smile on his face.

Chapter 19

Kate McLaren had waited a few hours before going down to Dom's, but had no trouble getting permission for Rick Hawke to come back to the station with her.

"Have I done something wrong already?" a perplexed Hawke said to Kate as they walked to the police car. "I've only been here a couple of days and I'm loving it. Have I upset Dom or someone?"

"No, nothing like that. We need to have a chat to you about something that happened overnight and we think it involves a returned veteran. Tony will explain it all when we get back to the station. We just want to pick your brain, that's all," Kate said sincerely as she drove.

Tony Signorotto didn't want Rick Hawke feeling nervous upon arrival so he made sure he met the car in the rear yard of the station. He motioned him to follow him through the back door and into a quiet room where Max Tyler was waiting. After shaking hands, Tony got straight to the matter in hand.

"Rick, we had a fatal shooting in Carlton last night and it involved someone we think was a returned veteran. It may be connected with another line of inquiry we have going at the moment. We are tracking this guy's dog tags through Victoria Barracks as we speak. We do have a name on him and I was wondering if you had heard of him at all. I think he's been rough sleeping like you," Tony said as he noticed Rick's face turn an ashen colour.

Rick Hawke grabbed for the nearest chair and sat down. Looking up slowly he began to speak with a very shaky voice.

"There were a few of us sleeping up at a church in Carlton. The Reverend up there was recently in Iraq, too. He contacted us somehow and offered us digs. Two are still there I think, but I got lucky with Dom's job and could get out. What was this guy's name?"

Max looked directly at Rick and spoke slowly.

"Billy McKay."

Hawke sat straight and threw his head back before placing both hands over his face.

"No, no, no. Not Billy. What the fuck happened?"

"You knew him then. Was he one of the ones up at the church?" Tony said quickly as he reached out and put a hand on Hawke's shoulder.

Hawke didn't say a word till after he had wiped tears from his face and composed himself.

"Yeah, he was. There was me, him, and another vet by the name of Ben Waite. Billy was a dope head and Ben's only got one leg after he took a hit over there. When did this happen?"

"Sometime last night or early morning up in Grattan Street. Can't go into a lot of detail but it looks like an execution style hit most likely with a nine-millimetre handgun. Some spent shells were found nearby at another shooting scene and we think there may be a connection between Billy's murder, the other shooting, and possibly a shooting a while ago involving another military target."

"I can't see any reason for hitting Billy. He's a junkie but harmless. Just another shattered returned veteran. He couldn't hurt anyone," a distraught Rick Hawke said.

"So Ben is still living at this church is he?" Max asked.

"Yeah. I was going to go up there and see how he was getting on. Especially after Jack Ziegler had a go at me at Dom's the other day. I was thinking that Ben and Billy would be finding it hard up there now that I've gone."

"Who is this Jack Ziegler?" Max said.

"He's this pastor or whatever that runs the church. He's ex-military and reckoned he served in Iraq with us as a minister. Your sergeant, Kate, saw him yell at me at Dom's. He didn't want me leaving the church, but I just wanted out. He's been taking church donations and giving them as handouts to us vets, which was starting to really piss some of his congregation off. I heard one of them accuse him of setting up some sort of quasi returned vets bed and breakfast. I think Billy and Ben needed him a lot more than me. Said we should all stick together and that the government was ripping us vets off."

"Let's get you a coffee and something to eat while we figure out what we can do for Ben." Tony Signorotto said, indicating to Max to take him into the mess room. "Get one of the troops to fix him up. We'll be with you in a few minutes, mate. Max, come on back as soon as Rick is looked after."

When Max returned a moment later, Tony turned to him.

"I don't like the possible direction this is going, Max. Returned vets and now one dead, together with a returned Minister who, by the sound of it, is pretty controlling and doesn't like the government for its inaction with the vets. I'm going to have a word with Kate seeing that she has seen this guy at Dom's. Max, get back in touch with Collins and Ethan Barnes and fill them in with regards to what Rick has said. We need to do two things straight away. First, find out from Rick where this church is and then get a welfare check done on Ben Waite. If you think he shouldn't be living there, then bring him out. He'll probably be pretty upset about his mate. I won't have this Jack Ziegler stopping him, and I reckon you need to interview him back here. Use that as a reason to get him out and we'll think of something to keep it that way."

"What are you thinking, Tony," Max said slowly.

"My nose tells me that something is not right here. We'll need to do a lot of digging. The dead one is a junkie and I hope this Ben isn't. We need a full story from him. Let's bring him in and then start sorting through what he knows about this church and Ziegler . I'm getting a search warrant too. The shootings all come back to a nine-millimetre of some sort."

Chapter 20

Jack Ziegler was no fool. He knew that McKay's death would come back to him somehow. He privately kicked himself for not removing Billy's dog tags. It wouldn't have solved the problem, but it would have given him more time. The questions from Ben Waite were coming thick and fast when he got back later that day after he took a detour via the Melbourne General Cemetery in College parade. He had made it over the fence without being seen and slipped the nine-millimetre pistol he had used on McKay down the side of a very old grave where the concrete cover had lifted. He had made a mental note of exactly where he placed it inside a heavy-duty plastic zip lock bag. After this he removed the hoody he was wearing and threw it into a nearby rubbish skip. When he had returned to the vestry he had also removed the New Testament where he had kept the gun hidden. He had walked back outside and put it down a gutter drain on the roadway. With a bit of luck no one would find it there.

"Where's Billy? The loud voice of Ben Waite had said as Ziegler passed by on the way to his own room after a quick shower.

"What do you mean. Isn't he here?" Ziegler said with an unconvincing voice.

Billy swung around on the old bed he had been lying on and reached for his metal crutch.

"You know damn well he's not. He followed you out of here hours ago and hasn't come back. Where is he?"

"I just went for a walk to try and compose next Sunday's sermon in my head. I didn't see him at all, mate. Just take it easy. He'll turn up," a lying Ziegler replied.

Ben was just about to mention that Billy had seen Ziegler with a pistol but suddenly thought better of it. Minutes later, sitting on his bed and sweating, he heard a loud banging on the front door. Sticking his head out, he saw Ziegler open the door and suddenly take a step back as several uniformed and plain clothes police entered the hallway.

"I am Detective Sergeant Tyler and this person with me is Inspector Nathan Barnes from the Federal Police. We are looking for a person by the name of Ben Waite. Is he here on these premises?"

Jack Ziegler just saw this as another example of authority raising its ugly head.

"Get off these premises. This is church property and you have no right to intrude here. Now get out," he yelled.

"And you are?" Nathan Barnes said holding up the Federal warrant to search.

"I am Reverend Jack Ziegler and this is my church and I'm asking you to leave. You have no authority here."

"That won't be happening, Pastor," Ethan Barnes replied as he indicated to several uniformed Federal police to spread out. "This is a Federal warrant to search these premises for evidence in relation to a murder. It supersedes anything the State of Victoria can do. This comes under the Counter Terrorism Act, 1993 and relates to all premises, including those of religious worship. Now how about answering the sergeant's first question. Is Ben Waite on these premises?"

With Ziegler about to say something, all heads turned to see a man on one crutch standing further down the hallway.

"I'm Ben Waite. Why do you want me?"

"You don't have to speak to them, Ben," Ziegler said very quickly.

Barnes and Tyler made a beeline for Waite. Barnes called for the other Federal police members he had brought along to commence the search.

"What are you looking for?" a now frantic sounding Ziegler called out.

Barnes indicated for one officer to stay with Ziegler.

"Take him into the kitchen and stay with him while the warrant is executed."

Ziegler was escorted away from them.

"Ben, I am Inspector Ethan Barnes from the Federal Police and my colleague here is Detective Sergeant Max Tyler from the Victoria Police. Do you know a Billy McKay?"

Waite quickly changed his stare from one member to the other and back again.

"Yeah, what's happened to him?"

"Why do you think something has happened to him, Ben?" Max Tyler asked quietly.

"He went out really early this morning to follow Ziegler for some reason," Ben said deliberately leaving out any mention of a pistol. He had a good idea of what he was about to be told about Billy, but he didn't want to get involved. He knew Billy was a hothead and should never have gone after Ziegler. "What's happened to Billy?"

"Billy's body has been found not far from here. He'd been shot."

At the same time as he felt a chill go through him with the news about Billy, he had no intention of telling either of these two that Billy had seen Ziegler with a pistol. He just wanted out of this church and away from Jack Ziegler.

"I think we have another mate of yours, Rick Hawke, at the station. He was the one who told us to come here. I don't think he has a lot of time for Ziegler. Do you want to see him, Ben?"

"Yes, if I could. What I would like more is to get out of here."

"We can take you to the station and then bring you back if you like," Barnes said.

"I don't want to come back here, but I've got nowhere else to go," a now distraught sounding Waite said.

"We will figure something out. Ben, let us worry about that," Max said, thinking of a future conversation he would have with Kate McLaren about Ben.

"Get your gear and come back to me, Ben," Max said as he looked at Ethan Barnes.

Fifteen minutes later, Ben Waite was ready to go to the Carlton Police station with strict instructions to the driver to keep him well out of the way of the watch-house area.

"Why's that, sarge?" the young Constable said as he went to escort Ben to the car.

"Because in a minute or so I'm about to load Jack Ziegler into another car for the same trip, only he'll be taken through the watch-house area to an interview room in relation to the possible murder of Billy McKay."

Chapter 21

Rick Hawke had asked to stay at the station when he was told the police were going up to Ziegler's church. He knew instinctively that if Ben was brought back, he would need all the support Rick could muster. At the end of the day, they were still a team, just like when they were back in the army. He sat in the mess room, drinking way too much coffee, but was glad that Kate McLaren was able to pop her head around the corner from her office to keep an eye on him.

After what seemed like an eternity, Ben walked slowly in on his crutches, with two police members behind him.

"Mate, sit down and we'll get you a coffee, and you can stay where it is warm and have a long chat to your friend here," indicating Rick Hawke, one of the members said.

Rick dragged his chair over to where a clearly shocked Ben Waite sat down.

"What the hell happened after I left, Ben?" Rick said with a low voice.

Ben turned to Rick with a confused look and spoke with tears in his eyes.

"Mate, Billy and I were thinking about getting out because Ziegler was starting to control us too much. Didn't want us doing anything he didn't know about. Last night, Ben decided to follow him. Billy had searched Ziegler's office and found a semi-auto pistol hidden in there. He told me about it, but what was I supposed to do with one leg and Billy back on the hard drugs again? I should have stopped him going after Ziegler. Now he's dead, and I'm back here."

"Ben, I've had some dealings with the people here, and I'm telling you that you can trust them. You've told them about the gun, haven't you?"

"No, no way. My nerves are bad enough without getting involved in this shit," a now even more distressed Ben said.

"You have to, Ben. Otherwise, he'll get away with Billy's murder."

"Billy was on smack when he went out after him. It's his own fucking fault he's dead," came the terse reply as Ben buried his head in his hands. "I'm not saying anything about the gun, okay? I'll tell them about what a strange dude Ziegler is, and that's all."

Rick Hawke stared at his dishevelled mate for what seemed like a minute, then hit him with a hard question.

"What are you going to do now? Where are you going to stay because you clearly don't want to go back there? I have digs because Tony and Kate from here have not only helped me with that but have also got me a job. You can't stay with me."

Ben Waite slowly looked up at Rick and said in a low voice between just the two of them, "I don't care anymore, mate. Might as well just top myself for all anyone cares. I'm a fucked-up nerve case. A one-legged returned vet who is useless."

Before Rick could reply, Kate McLaren spoke from the doorway, surprising both of them.

"You're not fucked up, and you're not alone, Ben. My partner Tom came back from over there after his wife was killed by a drunk driver. He's back on the cycle of life and is running a big security firm. No reason why you can't get it back together just like Rick here. He's not doing anything huge, but he feels better because he wants to get back in control of his life. Isn't that right, Rick?" Kate said with a wide-eyed look at Rick, hoping he'd back her words up.

"Kate and Tony have got me digs and a job with a friend of theirs who runs a restaurant in Lygon Street. I'm just washing dishes and generally helping out, but Christ, I feel better for it. It won't take you long to get back on the bike, but you've got to help yourself."

"I didn't hear what you two were talking about before I barged in, but if you like, Tom and I could help you out with a short-term stay at our place. We've got a bungalow down the back yard which could do with a clean out. It's got the basics: toilet, shower, bed. Comes complete with one of our old members from here who lives next door. She'd love you to help out with her garden and such. Her husband died about six months ago, and she's finding the yard and that a bit of a strain. Even with one leg, I'm sure you could help out. What do you say?" Kate said, thinking at the same time that she'd better prepare Tom about having a veteran move in.

Rick put his arm around Ben's shoulder at the same time as looking at Kate.

"Think we might have fallen on our feet here, mate. You finish your coffee, and I'll have a quick word with this lovely lady here. I could help get you moved in today if that's okay with Kate and Tom?"

"Thanks so much," Ben said, wiping tears away as Rick and Kate stepped out of the doorway to speak.

"He's scared stiff of everything at the moment, Kate. His nerves are shot, and I'm telling you that he said Ziegler had a gun. He didn't see it, but that's why Billy followed him last night. Did they bring Ziegler in for questioning?"

"They're about to question him in the front interview room. I've got to tell them about this before they start," Kate said as she began to walk away.

"It's going to take a lot to get Ben to say anything. Like me, Kate, he's had enough of guns and violence."

"Let's see how we go with Pastor Ziegler, shall we?" Kate said.

Chapter 22

Kate McLaren caught Max Tyler as he was about to enter the interview room and relayed to him the fact that Jack Ziegler had been seen with a pistol before he had been followed out of the church grounds.

"Where did this come from, Kate?" Max said quickly as Ethan Barnes beckoned him into the room.

"One very scared witness by the name of Ben Waite who is sitting in our mess room. He told Rick Hawke about it but won't back it up by telling us."

"Right," Max said, entering the room and quickly calling Barnes outside.

"Kate has just told me that Ben Waite was told by Billy McKay that Billy saw Ziegler with a firearm, but Ben is way too scared to say anything," Max said quietly. They both re-entered the room.

"You can't search religious premises for any reason," Ziegler said with a raised voice.

"I can under Federal firearms laws," Barnes replied. "This is a Federal warrant to search your church and surrounding land for weapons, and it remains in force for twenty-four hours. Do you understand that?"

With a very calm voice, a now seemingly relaxed Ziegler replied,

"Why are you searching for a firearm? I don't have guns on my church grounds," Ziegler said with a clear conscience now that he had hidden the pistol in the cemetery, and it became obvious that they hadn't found anything in their search.

"We are looking for a firearm that is possibly linked to the death of Billy McKay and the bullet damage to the military premises nearby to where his body was discovered."

A now crestfallen Ziegler looked from one police officer to the other before speaking.

"Oh my God. Has Billy been killed? What are you saying?

Why are you telling me now instead of back at the church? Does Ben know?" he said with all the conviction of an experienced actor.

"Yes. Billy was found earlier this morning not far from your church. He's been shot with a nine-millimetre pistol," Barnes said whilst noting that Ziegler's act was good, but his eyes were like two dead pools. There was no emotion behind them.

"I am so sorry to hear that. He was a struggling veteran who deserved so much more. What do you think happened, Inspector? He, along with Ben and Rick, were living up at my church. My parishioners were right behind their efforts to get back on their feet and get back into the society which had shunned them," a stony-faced Ziegler lied.

"Why had society shunned them?" Max quickly replied.

Jack Ziegler could not resist such a wide-open comment. This was his moment to get people to listen to him.

"More the military than the whole of society," he said with a voice that was starting to sound like it was coming from a church lectern where he had a captive audience. "These men have fought for their country and come home to be treated by the authorities with contempt. They put their lives on the line and should be treated as heroes. Instead, they have come back to closed doors."

Ethan Barnes took the questioning straight back to Ziegler with his next line, hoping that with anything Ziegler said, it could put a hole in his story.

"What authorities are you talking about exactly?"

Ziegler's mouth opened, and Barnes almost held his breath waiting for Ziegler to mention the Department of Veteran Affairs. The trap fell short.

"The medical people who they have been sent to for both physical and mental problems. They are all just lumped together and end up on a merry-go-round of appointments and drugs. All these people are getting a fee from the Commonwealth government, so they are shoved from one doctor or shrink to the next while these departments make hundreds of dollars from bulk billing. They don't care about the likes of Billy, Ben, or Rick. It's just a number to them. It should be stopped, and some real help and care given to them," Ziegler said with an increasingly aggravated voice.

"Who do you think is to blame for these downfalls that you are talking about?" Max said with the hope that Ziegler might take the bait and start on the Department of Veteran Affairs. The trap fell short again.

"The buck stops with Canberra. The process takes too long to get them back into society."

Ethan Barnes jumped in with the next comment.

"These men have all their money entitlements and do get medical care and even rent assistance at very generous rates from what I have been told."

"Who told you that rubbish, Inspector?"

It was the last chance saloon time now.

"Actually, a good friend of mine who works in the Department of Veteran Affairs."

Ziegler could not contain himself when he heard those words.

"Ah, the masters that send these lads to their deaths in some godforsaken place and then expect them to come home and be normal. Who's your insane friend there, eh Inspector?"

"Actually, Peter Galbraith. The head of Veteran Affairs," Barnes said with a straight face.

If looks could kill, Ethan Barnes would have been dead instantaneously. Ziegler's face had turned a shade of motley purple.

"The puppet master himself," Ziegler said with spittle coming out of his mouth.

Max Tyler could see what Nathan Barnes was doing, and it had succeeded. Barnes had thrown Ziegler's world off its axis. Now was the time to upset him even more.

"Well, from having three veterans staying at your church, you now have none," Max said with a blank look on his face.

"Ben is still staying up there," Ziegler said as he sat back in his chair.

"Oh, didn't I mention it? On the way back here to the station, he decided he wanted somewhere else to live. A bit like Rick Hawke. That church set-up doesn't really bode well for them. Now, as we are going back up there with our all-day search warrant, I'll get some of the Federal boys to get the rest of his gear and bring it back here. Why don't we get going again?" Max said.

"Why do you want to search again?" Ziegler said.

"We have some more information that we'd like to act upon," Max said quietly.

Jack Ziegler placed his hands behind his head and replied,

"Knock yourself out, officers."

Chapter 23

Tony Signorotto didn't like it. In fact, he not only didn't like it, but he was also feeling decidedly left out of it.

As he sat down for a coffee in the mess room, he was beginning to feel as though his world was spinning like a merry-go-round and he was about to be flung off it. Although he had been fully briefed on the ongoing situation with Jack Ziegler and the shootings, he was starting to believe he was only being given lip service by Ethan Barnes and James Collins. Lip service with a smile and a nod, with the occasional phone call thrown in. It was time for this to stop.

Leaning across the mess room table, he called out to one of the Constables who had just got up from having something to eat.

"Nip upstairs and tell Senior Sergeant McLaren that I want to see her down here, please. What's more, if Sergeant Tyler is there, tell him I want him down here also."

"I think he's still here, boss, but he's probably tied up with the shooting," the young member said. Signorotto slammed his cup down, slopping hot coffee onto the table. The young Constable took a backward step. Tony reined in his temper before he spoke.

"Just do what you've been told, thank you, Constable," he said through gritted teeth.

The young member picked up on his boss's vibes immediately and shot out of the room. Minutes later, Kate McLaren and Max Tyler walked in. Before they could speak, Tony got in first.

"Sit down, both of you. I've got something to say," the red-faced Signorotto said slowly. They did as they were told.

"What is my rank here?" he said, looking from one member to another just before Kate and Max looked at each other with puzzled looks on their faces. Kate took the lead.

"Er, Senior Sergeant, Tony. Is that what you meant?" she said nervously, knowing the Italian temper of her mentor could flare up pretty quickly.

"That's right, Kate. What I want to know is what is the difference between my rank of Senior Sergeant and your Senior Sergeant's rank here at the station?"

Kate knew where this was going. "You are the Senior Sergeant in charge, Tony. I am the sub-charge. What seems to be the problem?" she said slowly and quietly so as not to set him off.

"I am not criticising you, Kate. You, Max, well you are just in and out of here on the investigation, but I want to let both of you know that I not only want to be kept up to complete speed on this situation with this Ziegler character, whom I believe is a God-bothering liar from what I've been told in passing. Because I've seen no paperwork about him, I also am letting you know that I don't care less about this bullshit approach from headquarters about me sitting back behind a desk. This fucking crap has happened on our patch, and I will, like it or not, be in the lead party on this. I am not some half-arsed boss who is happy to let the bloody Feds run the show. Are we all on the same page with what I am saying?"

Before either Kate or Max could reply, a two-man crew appeared through the mess room door, chatting loudly to each other. They were not 'reading the room.'

"Out of here now," Tony barked as one of the members walked into the back of the front member who had been stopped in his tracks by the severity of the words. "Close the bloody door on the way out and tell everyone out there that Senior Sergeant Signorotto is in conference. Move."

The two members moved quicker than an Exocet missile, quietly closing the door behind them. Kate McLaren spoke straight up.

"Hey, Tony, settle down. Everyone here knows you are the boss. No need to yell at those two."

Max Tyler was gobsmacked by Tony's attitude and didn't know what to say. Silence engulfed the room for a good ten seconds before Tony spoke again.

"Okay, okay. But you two, of all people connected with this place, know where I'm coming from. I feel like this whole shit show is going on around me without any direct involvement, and I don't like it."

"Tony, it's not our fault the hierarchy have told you to sit on your hands until you're ready for the street again," Max said with genuine concern in his voice. "You know how glad everyone is just to have you back in the building." Tony looked at them with resolve.

"I'll settle this with the Superintendent on the phone right now. I am good to go as far as inquiries on the street with this matter. Kate, get on your computer and book me in ASAP with the Academy for a pistol shoot. I am either back or I'm out of here. By that, I mean the fucking job," he said as he stood and walked quickly towards the door, which he nearly wrenched off its hinges on the way out. Kate and Max looked apprehensively at each other at the same time as both exhaled loudly.

"Christ, Max. He'll give Collins an earful and won't take no for an answer. What is it with him?"

"He's not going to be just half a cop, Kate. He's either in or he's out, and hang the consequences. He's worked Carlton most of his career, and he's not going to let Ethan Barnes take over. You know what he thinks of the Feds. Good for looking after government buildings and that's about it. Old school and will go out living by the sword or dying by the sword."

"Don't say those words. Susie will have kittens if she finds out about him trying to hit the streets again," Kate said, wringing her hands.

Both members shook their heads slowly.

Chapter 24

Tony Signorotto had thought about fixing the situation he found himself in by making the appropriate phone call, but he knew that wasn't his way. He was old school, and this had to be done face to face. It was the only way he really knew.

One hour later, he stood in the office doorway of Superintendent James Collins at Police headquarters. Seeing that Collins had his head down over his computer, Tony knocked lightly on the door, forcing Collins to raise his head with a surprised look on his face.

"Tony, come in, come in. This is a surprise. What's up?" he said with no sign of a pending question in relation to Tony being out of the office.

"I've got to talk to you about my 'station only' situation. That's it in a nutshell. I'm not going to piss you around with this, but it isn't going to work, boss. I'm not one of those glass-half-full guys," Tony said with a straight face.

"Sit down to start with. No ceremony in this office," Collins said, indicating the couch to the side of his desk. Tony walked across and sat down and was surprised to see Collins get up and come across and take a seat next to the couch. Tony was obviously not comfortable with the seating arrangement and looked furtively around the office as he began to squirm slightly from side to side. Collins burst out laughing as he took his seat.

"For Christ's sake, mate. It isn't a psych's couch. Relax," he said as he picked up an internal phone.

"I want a plunger of *Vittoria* coffee and two cups in here, thanks, and while you're at it, some decent biscuits. I've got a real copper in here who needs real coffee. None of that powdered shit. Also, unless it's the Chief, I am not to be disturbed at all. Divert my phone also," Collins said, leaning back in his chair. "I think I might know why you've come in, Tony. First question from me, though, is what date have you got for your qualifying shoot at the Academy?"

"How did you know about me making a booking?" A very surprised Signorotto replied.

"If you're down as 'station only', mate, you are red-flagged at the range controller's office. It has to be approved by your Superintendent before you can bob up there waving a shooter around," he said with a laugh.

"Well, no point giving you a date then. Your Staff Officer would have cancelled it, eh?" A disappointed Signorotto said as he thought to himself that the trip in to town was now a waste of time.

"That sort of phone call comes straight through to me, not my staff officer, and so you don't go having a heart attack on me, I've ticked you off to go and have a shoot. Does that brighten your day?" Collins said.

"Well, thanks," a now dubious Signorotto replied. "What's the catch? If I qualify, do I just get to carry one around the office?" Tony said with a slight smile crossing his face.

"No bloody way, mate. You are more dangerous to everyone just hanging around your desk, especially with a gun. Believe me, I know. I haven't left you there without making daily inquiries about your welfare with members who shall remain nameless. You are too valuable to me for that. This shooting spree is too big a thing to leave you out of the loop on any point. I've already flagged your return to general duties because I need your local knowledge of Carlton, and not just from behind a desk. You give me the date of your Academy shoot, and after that, you are good to go. This is all on one proviso, though."

"There's always a bloody catch with you officers, isn't there?" A now fully smiling Signorotto said. "What is it?"

"I want a phone call from your wife Susie so I can explain to her why I'm letting you back on the street, which, by the way, will also be subject to teaming up at all times with another member, and by that, I mean a senior member."

Tony stood up at the same time as Collins. It was a case of two iron wills staring at each other, and Signorotto knew he wasn't going to win any more points in the conversation.

"My part's easy compared to yours," he said.

"What do you mean?" A curious Collins said.

Tony smiled as he slowly shook his head from side to side.

"Be ready for that phone call because you are going to get your ears pinned back."

Chapter 25

Three days later, Tony Signorotto was seated at the head of the station boardroom table. He had called for a meeting with the people he wanted for the investigation into the murder of Billy McKay. Around the table were Ethan Barnes, Max Tyler, Kate McLaren, and himself. There was no sign of any outsiders.

"First off, everyone, I am now, as of yesterday, fully re-qualified as firearm training goes, and as such, and after a rather lengthy and somewhat loud conversation between my lovely wife Susie and Superintendent James Collins, back on deck as to the running of the shooting side of this rather complex case is concerned."

"Ethan and I have had a meaningful discussion about who runs what from now on in. The trouble was, as far as I was concerned, that Ethan was covering the attempted shooting of Peter Galbraith and the shooting-up of the military establishment on our patch, which was perfectly right because Galbraith and the Melbourne University barracks are, if you like, Federal property, which he has jurisdiction over. I fully support him in this, but we also have the killing of Billy McKay, the retired veteran soldier who was killed on our patch of Carlton.

We are going to base all of these investigations out of Carlton. This room here will be set up as an ongoing base where both Ethan and I can call in our various experts when we want."

"Kate, I have spoken to Superintendent Collins, and he has decided that I will concentrate on Billy's death, along with Max here and any other CIU personnel that we think we need. You will be running the station as the In-Charge Senior Sergeant and being the conduit of any information that comes through the door. Are we all okay with this?"

Signorotto was greeted with nodding heads.

"The reason Collins hasn't got the Homicide guys on board fully is that we here at Carlton know the lay of the land.

Everything has happened in Carlton so far. Okay, if Galbraith hadn't lived in Carlton, then he may still have had a hit on him elsewhere, but the shooting-up of the barracks and Billy's death have happened within spitting distance of each other, which, correct me if I'm wrong, smacks of someone who has walked or run from all three incidents. If you were only going to shoot up the barracks, it would have been done in a drive-by shooting. Max, you want to keep going?"

"Thanks, boss. You're right, I think. Now that we have located where Billy was staying at the church, and given that Rick Hawke and Ben Waite have gotten themselves away from Jack Zeigler, I think it is fair to say that Ziegler is our number one priority as the possible shooter. Trouble is, Ben is too scared to say anything about what he has seen at the church, so we have a lot of work to do. Ethan, over to you."

"Thanks, Max. First off, I think our combined approach and information sharing will be the way all this is solved, and hopefully with the efforts we put in, it will stop any further instances. One of the top priorities about this going forward is that there will be absolutely nothing released about the shots fired at the regiment building or about Billy's murder. We need to see if this forces the hand of the killer in any way. Zeigler looks like he is the main suspect, but at this stage, we are lacking any substantive proof. Tony and I have been looking into Ziegler's past and are about to interview a few of his parishioners. We are going to leave him out of it on purpose for the time being, but when he hears that he is a person of interest, it might shake him up a bit. I believe you are going to tag him for a while, Tony?" Barnes said in the direction of Tony Signorotto.

"Yep, I've got Johnny Petran from the Regional Crime Unit teed up with a few of his boys to start a round-the-clock watch on Ziegler. To me, this character comes across as really strange. We know he's an ex-army padre that, according to some sources at Victoria Barracks in St. Kilda Road, has been shouting long and hard at the Federal Government for more funding, both financially and medically, for our returned vets. I have no problem with that, but we know he has left some very vitriolic messages with a lot of people down there. Since Max brought him into the station, Ethan and his people have been checking him out twenty-four seven, both here and in Canberra." Barnes then continued.

"We aren't placing all our eggs in one basket here. Ziegler is certainly up the top of our list, and as I said, we have a lot of interviewing to do with his parishioners and others. We've found out through Vic Barracks that he is a registered pistol shooter at the Melbourne Pistol Club in Fisherman's Bend, so I thought that, seeing you are a member down there, Kate, you might want to have a word with the Range Controller and see if you can find out anything. I know you are going to be busy, but we want you to keep in touch with Dom Santino at his restaurant in regard to Rick Hawke and how he is going. I believe you may also have somewhere for Ben Waite to stay in the short term?"

"No problem with keeping tabs on Rick. He is so grateful for the job, let alone the accommodation at Dom's, that he is really getting his act back together. Regarding Ben, my partner Tom Cole, who is also a returned veteran, has agreed with me to put him up for a while in a bungalow at the back of our place in Carlton. It's completely self-contained, and Tom is trying to arrange some work for him through a few contacts. In case you didn't know, Ethan, Tom is the General Manager of a very big security firm. I think he may be able to get him something close by in a cleaning capacity or such."

"The thing about Zeigler is that he hasn't seen me, so I was thinking that I might get a bit of religion from him," Tony said, looking at the others with a sly smile.

"What on earth are you talking about?" Kate said with a bemused look on her face.

"I'm going to join his parish throng and do some digging on him."

Chapter 26

Jack Zeigler was furious that there had been no headlines in any of the papers about the shots he had fired at the Melbourne University Regiment. There wasn't even anything about Billy's shooting. He felt nothing about killing him, but he knew he was going to have to not only be very careful in his future movements, but he was determined more than ever to bring the Federal Government to justice. If it meant forming his own little Waco, Texas-style set-up, then so be it. He had his church, and he was constantly trying to figure out ways to bring more returned veterans into his enclave. After all, he had God on his side, so there would be no stopping him, and if they thought that the Melbourne University Regiment had seen the end of him, they were wrong. The building was the entrée. Their Colonel-in-Chief, Simon Forbes, would be the main course.

Zeigler knew that he had to do his holy work soon on behalf of those men that had returned home from their duties abroad. He was not a stupid person, and although he had worked as a chaplain in war zones, he was well aware of the situations some of whom he considered 'his flock' had been placed in. He had concluded that the Iraq war would never be solved with overseas troops there. He had sent email after email to the military powers stating how futile the whole situation was and that it was just affecting the mental state of the Australian combatants. It was the same for all countries involved. The war in Afghanistan had never been won, and these overseas continuing conflicts should be left alone. The thought that these countries were actually acting as a deterrent to further genocide never entered his mind. He was at war with God and his country more and more as his deployment lengthened, and someone had to stand up for the troops.

Things started coming to a head when the military commander of the base that Zeigler was the chaplain for had been shown that the amount of troops reporting sick with mental conditions was severely affecting the battalion's strength. Upon sending investigators to the several military psychiatrists who were under his command, a pattern of reporting sick became glaringly obvious in that over ninety percent had been referred to them by Chaplain Jack Zeigler.

When Zeigler had been told to report to Brigade headquarters regarding the matter, he had refused to attend because, as he stated in an email, he worked for God, not the military. After a brief but fiery exchange of words with the base Commander, where Ziegler was told that he may think that he worked for God, but the military paid his wage whilst he was deployed, he had hung up the phone.

One week later, he was given his orders to return to Australia, where his position as a military chaplain would be immediately reviewed. Ziegler knew the military machine well. This meant he was subtly being told to resign or to be de-mobbed. If the latter happened, then he would find it very hard to find a civilian posting to a church back home.

He subsequently, days later, handed back his commission as a military pastor to the captain of the C-17A Globemaster transport aircraft that was about to lift off from al-Asad Air Base in Anbar province. He received a smiling, lukewarm salute in return.

Although he thought it might be hard getting a posting within his church upon his return, it was, in fact, the opposite.

The older pastors in the Church of the Uniting Spirit were retiring one after the other, and new blood was needed in several locations. Ziegler had always loved the cosmopolitan attitude of the inner Melbourne suburbs of Carlton, Collingwood, and Fitzroy, so when the Parish of Carlton in Palmerston Street was offered to him, he grabbed it with both hands for two reasons. The first being the location and the atmosphere, and the second was that he knew he could attract some returned veterans who had problems to his new church. Through word of mouth from working at a few of the late-night soup kitchens around the CBD, he started to pick up names of the rough sleepers that had served. That is where he had, to his mind, 'recruited' the likes of Rick Hawke, Billy McKay, and Ben Waite. He had gotten them off the streets with promises of the possibility of some employment and a roof over their heads. To Ziegler's thinking, this was the beginning of his own army.

Ziegler began using the church as a cover for his own retribution against the military. He actually thought he was on a mission from God when he attempted to kill Peter Galbraith. He now believed that the two veterans who had deserted him were on his list of enemies. When he was giving sermons from the church pulpit, he referred to himself as the 'returned military chaplain' and never as a pastor.

The congregation of the Church of the Uniting Spirit were beginning to talk amongst themselves about this fiery person. At first, the fire and brimstone sermons attracted quite a crowd, but as weeks and then months wore on, it became obvious that this man had a fixation with the military. Even when some of the parishioners questioned him about his attitude against the Government, they were told that 'God demanded justice for the veterans.'

After almost a year as head of his church, the pews were emptying out, but Ziegler didn't care.

His rage against the Machine of War was about to escalate to a point of no return. As he stepped into his pulpit during his Sunday service, he didn't seem to notice the new face towards the back of the sparse attendees.

Tony Signorotto sat there in scruffy clothes with a three-day growth of beard and settled in for the former Sky Pilot to speak. What he heard spew from Ziegler's mouth was a litany of abuse aimed at anything military, but more so towards anyone in charge of anything military. The one place Signorotto thought of was the St Kilda Road army headquarters. That place had full-time officers working there.

What Jack Ziegler was thinking about in his vitriolic sermon was an establishment closer to home.

Chapter 27

Kate McLaren took a sip from her coffee before she addressed the rest of the team sitting around the table.

"Well, I've been to the Melbourne Pistol Club and spoken with the head range controller. He showed me the pistol that Ziegler keeps there, and it isn't a nine-mil Smith and Wesson. It's a ten-mil Glock K20G4 15-shot, so it definitely isn't the pistol used to kill Billy McKay. He says that Ziegler hasn't been down to shoot for a couple of weeks, and he showed me the sign-in book to verify it. I know they run a very strict club because I've been a member of it for a few years now, and they abide by all the laws and rules tightly. So if he is our killer, the thing we have to realise is that he is using another firearm. The shots at Galbraith, the Melbourne Uni regiment, and Billy's killing were all from the same gun, a nine-mil Smith and Wesson."

Tony Signorotto looked from Kate to Max and then to Ethan Barnes before speaking.

"Okay, well we conducted a full search of that church and the presbytery, and we came up with nothing. If Ziegler is our man, and he wants to keep on going with his plan, whatever it is, then we are going to have to cover him twenty-four seven. I know we have the Regional Crime Unit, but I think we are going to have to help them out with some of our own uniforms. Anyone got any other ideas?" Max Tyler indicated to speak. "Go ahead, Max."

"There's one area I think we have to push harder on. Ben Waite is now living at the back of Kate and Tom's place, and he has had time to realise he doesn't have to have anything to do with Ziegler any more. He needs to be questioned again because I'm sure he knows more than what he is telling. He was at the church the night Billy went out, and he won't talk about it. I reckon he either saw something that night or Billy did and told him, and now he's too scared to say anything. Kate, how's he been since he's been at your place?"

"He's been good. Doesn't say much though. Tom got him some part-time work cleaning at one of the places where his security company has a contract. Got him three days a week and seems to be happy with it. I think, though, that if you want to speak to him about anything like what you are suggesting, then maybe take him for a coffee at Dom's and sit down with Rick Hawke. I know Ben looks up to Rick, so he might open up. If he does know something about Zeigler, it might shortcut our search for the killer."

"Good idea, Kate," Ethan Barnes said. "Max and I have been trolling through the records of any returned veteran we think is noteworthy. I also spoke at length to his former commanding officer, and he told me about all the troops that went off with stress or mental issues while Ziegler was the Chaplain. Looks like the good Chaplain had quite a lot to say about the Army in general and the way the troops weren't looked after. In the end, Ziegler was sent home and resigned his commission and disappeared back into civilian life. According to the Army shrinks, there had been heaps of personnel that had been influenced by Ziegler to chuck it in while they were over in Iraq."

"Not only looking more and more as a chief suspect, but more and more as a bloody radical nutter. If we can arrange that coffee for tomorrow morning, I'll come with you, Max," Tony said.

Chapter 28

Jack Ziegler's ego had spent most of the night at a food van in the city, helping to nourish the city's homeless. At least, that was what his ego was doing, but in actual fact, he was on a recruiting mission to keep justifying his fight against the Federal Government by getting some more returned veterans under his wing, and bringing them to his church in Carlton.

He scoured the alleyways around the inner city and chatted to anyone who was sleeping rough. He also asked them the one question he wanted answered, and that was: did they know anyone in their position who was a returned veteran? He was directed to one bedraggled man, but when he gave him a packet of sandwiches and asked him where he had served, he was immediately kicked and punched by him. Ziegler only wanted compliant veterans, who he believed he could recruit into his world of revenge—those who, after some time with him, would be his helpers with his cause. The last type he needed was one who could draw attention to his church. He knew that, even at the moment, his parishioners had been sending emails to the Bishop, requesting his removal after the police visit. He kept up his quest right through to the morning, but thought constantly about Rick Hawke and his abandonment. Ben Waite had removed himself, but probably wouldn't have if the police hadn't interfered. Billy McKay wasn't even given a thought. He decided just to go back and have a sleep for a couple of hours, then go to that café in Lygon Street to confront Hawke about his traitorous behaviour.

Upon getting home, he took a Ritalin and a Modafinil tablet in the confused hope that it would aid in a few hours' sleep. He had been prescribed both by a local doctor, but had been told not to take them together. The use of both of these drugs separately was meant to help with motivation and cognition. Combined, they were only going to hype Ziegler up and make him confrontational, but then God's messenger was not to be ignored.

***

Rick Hawke had just finished a cup of coffee at Dom's restaurant before starting work. He was really appreciating the calmness in his life now, and it was all down to Dom Santino and his lovely wife, Maria. The fact that he lived above the restaurant meant he didn't have to battle the chaos of Melbourne's transport system, and the work, although mundane, was quite therapeutic. He was getting himself back on his feet and loved his daily chats with Dom and Maria. Life wasn't perfect, but he knew it was a lot better than living back in the church with Ziegler. He turned to Dom, who was just opening the front door of the famous Lygon Street eatery.

"I'll get the tables for the footpath, Dom. Leave it with me."

Dom Santino liked having Rick around. Not only was it good for the safety of his restaurant to have him living there, it was also nice to be able to talk to him during the day as they both went about their work. Dom's life was surrounded by his wife, Maria, and his daughters, Gina, Rosa, and Silvana, who dropped in constantly either after their work or on the weekends. It was a truly Italian affair, and he would have it no other way. The Italian way was family, and that was all that mattered.

Rick Hawke was arranging the tables and the outdoor heaters when a shadow loomed large across the red-and-white-checked tablecloth that he had just placed down. The next thing he knew, a voice boomed in his ear. He quickly turned to see a very agitated Jack Ziegler. Rick noticed immediately that Ziegler's pupils were like pinpoints and that he couldn't keep from bouncing around from one foot to another, like some doped-up prize fighter.

Ziegler might have frightened Ben Waite and even Billy when he was alive, but he didn't scare Rick, who had seen soldiers like this in Iraq. He had resisted the flood of illegal amphetamines that worked their way into the army camps, but he knew the irrational behaviour of drug use when he saw it. He stood up, but deliberately didn't say anything to provoke or agitate Ziegler, who started to speak in a loud voice.

"I picked you up off the scrapheap, Hawke, and you just walked out on me and my church. You owe me, Rick," Ziegler said, as he shuffled around in front of Hawke.

"I owe you nothing, Ziegler," Hawke said in a low, controlled voice, as he noticed three men take seats at one of the tables. "How about you just go away before you do something you'll regret? There are customers here now, so just go."

Ziegler stepped in front of Hawke as he approached the three tough-looking men who were waiting to give their order. Rick didn't need to take their coffee orders, in reality. These three men were Mafiosi, and regular customers at Dom's, and they had the standing order of three short black coffees at the same time every day. They weren't people to be messed with. They had respect for Dom and his family, and had frequented Dom's for years. They always sat fronting Lygon Street and had a three-hundred-and-sixty-degree view of anyone or anything that was approaching them. People like Ziegler were laughed at by these types. Ziegler made a bad mistake by yelling at Rick.

"Forget those three there," Ziegler said, indicating the three men, who were now giving him the coldest stares they could. "You listen to me, Hawke. You are a returned veteran who is manipulated by the Government. A Government that fobs you off with a measly pension. We need to show that they aren't doing enough. I will show them though. I am rising up to take them on. I will stop them from sending more soldiers."

Hawke tried to step around Ziegler again to get to the customers. Once again, Ziegler moved to block him. One of the three black-suited Mafiosi spoke to Hawke.

"You are a veteran?" To which Hawke nodded. "Then I suggest you just get us our coffees. We will look after this person," indicating Ziegler.

"Please, no trouble. He's not worth it," Hawke said as he turned and went into the restaurant. The other black suits stood, and all three approached Ziegler. The first one spoke again.

"You have made two mistakes, my friend. The first is that you have interrupted our morning coffee, and the second is that we have a lot of time for our returned soldiers, so we suggest you just go right now. Eh?"

Ziegler stepped into the personal space of the three men, just as a fist hit his stomach like a pile driver, sending him to the ground. Because of the drugs he had taken, he bounded straight back up and started to throw punches at the three. He had no fear. As he went down in a hail of counter-punches, Rick Hawke and Dom Santino came running out onto the footpath.

"Stop, stop," Dom implored, just as the drug-enhanced Ziegler went to throw a swinging punch at the restaurateur.

The wild punch was blocked not by any of the three men, nor Rick Hawke. Ziegler's arm was violently twisted up his back, and he was shoved face-first over a table by Tony Signorotto, who had just walked around the corner with Max Tyler and Ben Waite. As the two police officers held the struggling Ziegler down, Tony turned to Dom, and, with a grin, spoke, nodding towards the three Mafiosi standing to one side but ready to give Ziegler a pounding.

"Dom, I think these gents would clearly like their coffees, eh?" The trio re-adjusted their ties and sunglasses, and quietly moved to their seats at the table. Tony knew them all through his Mafiosi uncle, Benny Illarietti, who, till a few years ago, had been the Don of the Mafiosi in Melbourne. Tony kept hold of Ziegler and gave a nod to the men as if to say that he was now in control of the situation. One of the three, a crime figure by the name of Alphonse Signori, nodded to Tony and indicated to his compatriots to take their seats and keep out of things. Rick grabbed Ben and hustled him into the café, unseen to Ziegler. Max Tyler had already called for police back-up before they grabbed Ziegler, so he and Tony strong-armed him around the corner and stood him against the wall.

"Bad mistake, Pastor. You just threw a punch at a person who is not only a good friend of all the police in Carlton, but also a very good *amico* of the black-suited brigade around here. I don't know what happened before I arrived, but I can tell you that I am going to charge you with assault."

"I didn't touch him," Ziegler screamed.

"You don't have to touch someone to assault them, Mr Ziegler. It's enough to put them in fear of being hit, and I'm quite sure the magistrate will see that." Just as Tony finished speaking, the Carlton Divisional Van screeched to a halt next to them. Calling the two van members over to him, he indicated for them to put Ziegler into the rear of the caged vehicle.

"Take him back to the station and hold him in an interview room. I don't care how much he kicks and screams, I've got to see someone back at the café, and Detective Sergeant Tyler has to take a statement from Dom. Off you go." The two members did as they were instructed, and Tony, together with Max, walked back to the café.

"Dom, I need a *caffè ristretto*, my friend. It's a while since I had a bit of action, so I want to sit and relax for a minute or two and sip one of your finest before having a chat to Rick and Ben about our friend who just left."

"*Caffè ristretto* coming up, my good friend," the still shaken Dom Santino said.

Chapter 29

No matter how many times or ways Tony Signorotto and Rick Hawke approached the subject of what Billy McKay saw or heard that night when he followed Jack Ziegler, there was nothing they could do as they sat in Dom's restaurant to convince him to give up anything useful in relation to the ex-Chaplain. Rick took Tony to one side as Max Tyler sat with the clearly upset Ben Waite.

"Tony, I've really got to get back to work. Customers are coming in and I need to be in the kitchen to help out Dom and Maria. I'll tell you this though, Ben is scared because even though I tried to get him out of the way of that fight, he still saw Ziegler for what he is. That bloke is unhinged."

"I know, I know." Tony said softly. "I think I'll let Kate work on him a bit back at her house. As the saying goes, softly, softly treads the monkey."

"Anyhow, you have to get back to the station and charge Ziegler with assaulting Dom." Hawke said in reply.

"No mate, I'm not going to charge him for a couple of reasons. First is that I don't want to drag Dom into court. I spoke to him before, and he just doesn't want to press charges. He reckons that if Ziegler had connected with that wild haymaker, then it might be a different story. Thinking it through, if I did charge him then his Bishop would most likely kick him out of the church and then we'd have no idea where he was going or what he was up to. I want to keep him on our radar. Much easier for boys who are shadowing him around the clock to keep tabs on him if he has a base."

"What are you going to tell Ziegler?" Rick asked.

"Just that Dom doesn't want to go ahead with assault charges. I don't want Dom or his family involved with this guy. The Santino's are family to me, and I won't have them put at risk," Tony said in a matter-of-fact tone as he stood to leave.

Approaching Ben, he patted him on the shoulder and got a very shaky look in return. "Be in touch, Ben. Sorry about today but you can see what we mean about Ziegler. He's obviously on meds and it's feeding his paranoia."

"Just need time to get my life back together, Senior Sergeant. Can't handle people like him at the moment. He just makes me think of when I served," Ben said flatly.

Max stood to go with Tony but as they stepped away, he turned back to speak.

"Billy served too, Ben. He paid the ultimate price. Maybe think of what you owe him," he said gently. "Come on, let's get you back to Kate's place."

"Talk soon Ben," Rick Hawke said turning towards the rear of the restaurant.

"Yes mate. Just a little bit of time."

"I just hope we have time with this idiot. He's a very dangerous unit," Tony said.

Tony and Max dropped Ben Waite back home. Tom Cole, Kate McLaren's partner, came out of the gate to meet the trio.

"You up for some work tomorrow, Ben? One of our clients down at a building site needs a guy to check the trucks coming in and out of the place. Be a long day but it's good pay."

"Sounds good to me, Tom. Thanks. Kate and you have been really kind to me since I came here," he said as he walked around the back of the Coles property to his bungalow.

"What's wrong with him? Did you get your information out of him about Ziegler?" Tom asked Tony.

"No, nothing. He saw a punch up involving the good pastor and a couple of black suits.

Had to arrest Ziegler in the end, but I think it put the shakes into Ben when he saw how quickly Zeigler flew into a rage."

"I'll work on him quietly from my end and let you know."

"Thanks Tom. We just want to drag Ziegler in with something concrete to pin on him regards the shootings."

Chapter 30

Jack Ziegler walked out of the Carlton police station with a grin on his face. He'd managed to see Ben Waite just as the fracas started, so now he knew that the police had basically removed he and Rick Hawke and taken them under their protective wing. He knew in his own mind that he had to let go of these two and look for other veterans to join him.

First things first though. He had to get back to what his main mission was and that meant he had to find another target connected to the military that was feeding the war machine. Even though there were no more military personnel being sent overseas at the moment, which could all change in an instant no matter what government was ruling the country. What made him smile to himself was that although he had a target, he also knew exactly what date he was going to go to war. April 25th. Anzac Day. The holy of holies in the minds of the ignorant people of Australia. The day they celebrated war.

He had one week to prepare so it was time to do more research. Knowing from experience that every member of all military establishments in the land would be out and about before dawn on that date, he would be lying in wait for his target.

As he walked back to his church, he was convinced that he was a 'person of interest' to the police at Carlton now, so he decided to go on the offensive by actually becoming more paranoid than he already was. He constantly looked around him for anyone that could be following him. Stopping and looking in shop windows for anyone coming to a halt near him and even doubling back on his walk would become normal for him now.

Getting to the entrance to his church he spun around and caught a fleeting sight of a male crossing the road about fifty metres back. He couldn't swear to it but the check shirt he saw the individual wearing looked just like one he had seen on the back of a man that was standing at a distance in the rear yard of the Carlton police station when he had been released. Paranoia had its benefits.

Once inside he opened up his computer and googled *Anzac Day military ceremonies-Melbourne*. Up came all the ceremonies that were to take place in the suburbs. He ignored all the ones that were going to happen at Returned Service League clubs and anything to do with the actual dawn service or ceremonies at the Shrine of Remembrance. Those events and even the actual march through the city held no interest for him. The last thing he wanted to do was become a martyr. He wanted to go on getting his so-called revenge on behalf of the veterans, never stopping for one moment to think that he was the only one wanting to take this path of actual murder. In reality it was because he was really given no choice but to leave the military and had borne a huge grudge against their establishment for what he had perceived they had done to him. The chip on his shoulder was now an all-encompassing path of life.

He narrowed down his search to what he knew in his mind would be his hit. He looked closely at the times of events happening at the Melbourne University Regiment. There was going to be a dawn service of sorts where the entire company of approximately fifty members were expected to attend. In that number was their Commander, Colonel Simon Forbes.

Ziegler knew how these Colonels operated. They weren't full time soldiers, and most hadn't even served overseas. They were, in general, all executive types in their own businesses who had been part of the old 'Home Guard' ever since their cadet days at private schools. Some were even doctors and lawyers who wanted to keep the old traditions up. They were all referred to by the mainstream military as 'weekend warriors.' He had previously been through all the usual social media tabs and trolled through LinkedIn until he had found him. Forbes was there as the CEO of a private hedge fund organisation that was probably worth millions. He had discovered all his high-class contacts and school mates from Scotch College on the corporate version of Facebook which was what LinkedIn actually was. It had taken no effort to find his home address in Leopold Street in South Yarra. These types never thought they needed security. He now had to put his deadly plan into action. The next thing he had to do was somehow sit off where he worked and follow him home. No way would Forbes be taking a train or tram home.

Jack Ziegler went upstairs and took a surreptitious look through the curtains and sure enough, check shirt man was sitting across the road sipping on a coffee at the outside seating area of the local café.

He would sleep on it tonight and think of how he could slip the tag from his followers and work his way to Windsor. He didn't own a car, but to his devious mind he knew he would come up with a plan. First thing in the morning was to go across the road and get a coffee and 'spot the cop.'

Settling down for the night, he made sure he had his Ritalin and Modafinil tablets ready for the morning. It would be an interesting first day of his master plan.

Chapter 31

Six days to Anzac Day

"Sorry guys. He just took off on me and there was only one there," one of the undercover team that was assigned to Ziegler around the clock muttered unconvincingly to the quickly gathered group in front of him at the Carlton police station.

Although he was not a Victorian Police member, Ethan Barnes could not help himself from questioning the member.

"Are you telling us that he got away from you. How?" Barnes said loudly looking around the table at Tony Signorotto, Max Tyler, Kate McLaren and the very embarrassed Johnny Petran, the Acting Sergeant in charge of the member telling the sorry tale.

"I had just swapped over with another member and was sitting down at the café opposite Ziegler's house. I didn't want to look out of place, so I'd bought a coffee and all of a sudden, he walks past me into the café. He had a good look around the few customers that were inside, but I don't think he spotted me sitting where I was. The only thing I could do was sit there with my coffee. A few minutes later he comes out with a takeaway and walks back past me. I turned around and watched him walk past an orange e scooter and through his gate," the red-faced member said.

"What then?" Tony Signorotto chipped in with knowing full well what the answer was going to be.

"The next thing I know he's back and on it and takes off down the footpath on the other side of the road. He accelerated away before I could even get up. I honestly thought he was just getting an early morning coffee."

"What did you do then?" Max Tyler said with a stunned expression. "Except watch him disappear?"

"Just called it in to Johnny here," the subdued plain clothes member said, indicating Johnny Petran whose facial expression and shaking head was one of total disbelief.

Tony Signorotto held up one hand and spoke.

"There's nothing we can do about it now Johnny, so get onto the company that owns those scooters. I think it is called Neuron. I want to know if they can give us details of where it went to. You have to use a card to pay for one and I know they have some sort of tracking device on them. We've been having all sorts of trouble with them being left on footpaths around Carlton. Give them Ziegler's name and see how much information they can give us. I know they share their data with the Melbourne City Council so check them too. Any trouble give them my name and tell them to ring me ASAP."

Johnny Petran walked quickly towards the office door, indicating to the member who had lost Ziegler to follow him. The pointed finger gave the member no option.

"We have no idea where he was going so we will have to wait on the information coming back," Kate McLaren said. "And if he does turn back up today at his church it's no good questioning him. If we ask him where he went on his scooter ride, then he'll laugh at us. I know I would if I was in his position."

"I'm going to have to give all this to Superintendent Collins," Tony said as he picked up his mobile phone. "It could all be innocent enough but the more we rake over Ziegler the more he smells."

"He hasn't gone back to his pistol club since we visited him at his church the other day and we know that the gun he keeps there isn't the one that killed Billy McKay which means that if he's our man then he has a nine mil Smith and Wesson hidden somewhere." Kate said.

Max looked at the others and spoke slowly.

"People, I've been giving this a fair bit of thought. Look at who and what's been targeted so far. We've got the attempted murder of the head of Veteran Affairs which happened in Carlton, the shooting up of the Melbourne University Regiment, once again in Carlton. The killing of Bill McKay, again in Carlton.

All military and all in Carlton."

"No news in that," said Ethan Barnes. "What are you getting at, Max?"

"I'll play the hunter then," said Max. "One miss with Vet Affairs, which hasn't gone public, one building with a few bullet holes in it, again no public interest and one killing which we've stopped from going public. I'd be getting a bit pissed off if I was him."

"Your point being?" Kate said.

"Well, If I was him, I'd want to grab some headlines and there is a time coming up quickly where someone will take note of him. We need to look at what's happening in Carlton next week on Anzac Day," Max said quietly.

Tony Signorotto looked up quickly with a startled expression on his face.

"People, we've got work to do. This is not going down here on that day. No fucking way!"

Chapter 32

Five days to Anzac Day

Jack Ziegler knew quite well that the e scooter would reveal not only how he paid for his ride but also where it started from and ended. He had been using this method of transport for any journey he had to make outside of Carlton. He wasn't going to leave it anywhere near his actual destination. What he was going to do though was draw a smokescreen across his path to keep any police trackers guessing.

Getting an early drop on those who may be watching him had been essential and he had kept a strict eye behind him as he travelled across the city and up St. Kilda Road towards the Shrine of Remembrance. Halfway along Birdwood Avenue he finished his ride and left the scooter and helmet neatly parked on the gravel pathway of the Tan. From there he set off on a brisk walk into South Yarra and the home address of Colonel Simon Forbes. The distance was nothing when you had popped a couple of Ritalin to help you on your way. He was on a mission.

At about eight forty-five that morning, he propped himself near a tree on the opposite footpath to number twelve Leopold Street, Forbes's address. The houses were small terrace style ones along the street but in the location where they were, all were valued around two million dollars or above, depending on their condition. Forbes's was no exception. It was in pristine condition. There were no garages attached to any of them, just little part driveways where the rich could nose or back in their Mercs, BMWs, or Range Rovers. In the driveway at number twelve was a BMW iX with the personalised registration plate SF3141. The arrogance of Forbes putting the postcode of South Yarra on his car would make this even more satisfying, Ziegler thought to himself.

Ziegler quickly walked across the road and ducked down

beside the car. On the back window was a military sticker with the silhouette of a soldier with the words underneath stating *I serve. Do you?* He shook his head and thought about how many people would actually pull up beside the vehicle, look at Forbes and think what a great Australian he was. Walking quickly back to the other side of the road, he stood behind the tree again and waited. He had seen a picture of Forbes before, but he wanted to make sure that when the time came in a few days that he had the right man. Ziegler had no compunction about what he had planned for this pathetic individual who basked in the glory of the uniform and war when he knew he had never stepped a military boot outside of Australia. In his mind this person was a total imposter. No mercy would be shown.

It wasn't long before a man came out of the front door of the house at number twelve. Ziegler had researched Forbes and there was no mention on any social media or LinkedIn account of him being married or having children. Forbes strode to his car wearing a very new-looking dark blue suit with a blindingly white shirt without a tie and carrying what was obviously an expensive shoulder bag. He unlocked the BMW with a beep from the hand-held key fob. Once inside he started the powerful vehicle and with a quick look both ways pulled out into the street and accelerated away.

From the expensive house in the expensive car to his well-healed job in Collins Street, Ziegler thought to himself. *I will be doing God's work here.*

Satisfied that he had eyed the correct person and having seen what he wanted, Ziegler headed off to St. Kilda Road to get a number sixteen tram back to Carlton.

Trams were obviously a bit mundane for Simon Forbes he thought.

Chapter 33

Four days to Anzac Day

Superintendent James Collins drove into the rear yard of the Carlton Police station almost at the same time that Johnny Petran did.

"What's the latest, Johnny?" Collins said as they both headed to the back door where Tony Signorotto was waiting. After greetings were shared, the three men went upstairs to the conference room. Ethan Barnes was in his office at Victoria Barracks working through logistic problems for the Anzac Day ceremonies and Max Tyler was in the city at a court hearing.

"I've got all the details about Ziegler's scooter trip. It might be something, might be nothing," Petran said as he reached for the permanently percolating jug of coffee by the far wall. He threw in a couple of sugars and began to tell the story.

"It seems all legit on the outside. All Neuron did when I went in was take the name, I gave them and sure enough everything popped up. We know he doesn't have a car so this must be his way of getting around. He has a long history with Neuron since they first got their scooters on the streets here. I personally think that..."

"Cut to the chase please Johnny. Just the facts," a terse Signorotto said curtly.

"Right, boss. Well, he runs a credit card with them, and his record of hire shows all the trips he takes on them. This one is down as him picking up the scooter outside the church like we knew and then it takes a more or less straight run through the city along Swanston Street, and he parks it up in Birdwood Avenue near the Shrine but not really close to it. If he's trying to get out of sight, he's done a good job. There's no CCTV in that area and I've checked all the footage closer up at the Shrine. Trouble is, because we are so close to the day itself there's a lot going on there what with scaffolding and the rest. Also heaps of people hanging around the area waiting to do Shrine tours and everything."

"What about any record of him getting a scooter back to Carlton." Collins said.

"Ahead of you there, boss. The ride into Birdwood Avenue is the last one recorded. Got onto Neuron very early this morning and he didn't get a ride back on one of their scooters." Petran said quickly.

"That's not to say he didn't use someone else's card though!" a frustrated Signorotto said as he picked up a phone and barked orders down the line for the watch house keeper to immediately chase up the Inspector-in-charge of the Shrine Guard and get the CCTV of the entrance to the Shrine tour for the applicable time frame. Seconds after he had put the phone receiver down, it rang. Signorotto picked it up. Before he could speak, Kate McLaren's voice came out of the speaker.

"Tony, the troops down here are flat out. You'll have to get someone else to run your errands for you. I know we are on a tight timeline what with Anzac Day coming up, but we still have a station to run downstairs, understand?"

Tony stood as he began to yell into the phone.

"Don't care, Senior Sergeant! This takes priority over some local punter's problem. Do you understand?" Slamming the phone down he turned to Collins and Petran. Before he could speak, Collins indicated to Petran that he should leave the room.

"You listen to me right now, Tony. I'm the one that got you back here against everyone's ideas, mate. Don't you dare mouth off to Kate about this shit. She has been running this place while you've been off sick, and she's done a brilliant job. I know you are stressed about Ziegler, but until we get some concrete proof that he is our shooter then I am not bringing him in just so you can have him tucked up in a cell for Anzac Day. Now do you understand where I'm coming from? If you don't come down a few notches with your temperament, then I'll have no choice but to put you back on the sick list and that means out of here okay."

Signorotto took a deep breath and walked over to the window and stared into the sky before slowly turning to face his Superintendent.

'It's all changing. Time was when you dealt with straight up crooks. There were rules out on the street. Well, sort of rules. If they crossed the line, they expected us to come down on them hard. No hidden agendas, no bullshit. All my career it was us against them and now look what you have," Signorotto said with emotion in his voice.

A concerned Collins looked at Signorotto. "What are you getting at?"

"We dealt with crims. Now look who we are dealing with. Guys who are pissed off with the Government of the day because they don't like the status quo. Take this guy Ziegler. Has a set against the military obviously and wants to take it out on the establishment and the people and places that protect us from what's wrong with the world. Christ sake, boss. It used to be a war against the Italian mafia, the Romanian mafia and the rest. Now we are fighting idealism. I'm finding it hard to get my head around this shit. Take when I went to his church and listened to him rant against what he reckons is the war machine. What happens to him? Absolutely fucking nothing. His parishioners send off a few emails with no replies coming back. We have idiots marching through the streets every weekend complaining against anything. If you ever asked one of them to step up and fight for this country, they'd run a mile before fighting for our freedom. Here we are looking at some half- baked religious nut riding around on a bloody electric scooter and probably laughing at us. What do we do? Check his fucking e scooter account for Christ's sake. This is all bullshit. Even ten years ago if someone looked like they might do something to upset Anzac Day they'd be hauled off the streets. Now they have fucking rights. What fucking rights do our Veterans have to protect them. Tell me that. Tell me please, cause I'm finding that I'm starting to live in some other world where everything is being turned upside down and to tell you the truth, I'm struggling big time with it."

Do I let him stay on this or do I drag him back to the company shrinks? Collins thought.

Collins turned to Signorotto and pointed towards the door.

"First things first, Tony. Get downstairs and apologise to Kate. Then go into the bathroom and have a good look at yourself in the mirror. I haven't known you all that long but this isn't the Tony Signorotto that I've been told about. The one who would defend his own no matter what. The one who would see any situation through. If I have to take you off this, you will be not only off it, but you will be back home and facing a long recovery with a lot of questions asked. I know it's a new type of situation away from the norm of day-to-day policing, but we are still dealing with a murderer, and he has to be stopped. You're the one who said he didn't want anything more happening on his patch so let's get this sorted."

Signorotto knew Collins was right. He was starting to think that maybe he had come back to work too soon. Maybe he was living on his nerves a bit too much That was the way he had always operated, but with this he felt that he was fighting an uphill battle. He walked past Collins then slowly down the stairs and fronted up to a very busy inquiry counter being manned by two uniformed members and overseen by Kate McLaren who glanced quickly at him and then kept helping to answer the everyday questions of the Carlton locals.

"Feel free to give us a hand here, boss," Kate said as he approached her.

"Just wanted to say…" Signorotto started but got cut off by Kate very quickly.

"All's forgiven. I know that you think going around attacking and killing people connected with the military is tantamount to attacking and killing police but that is the world we are living in unfortunately. Come over here and get back to some normality."

Signorotto stepped up behind the counter and looked at the everyday faces of the United Nations of Carlton and realised this was what policing was really about.

I think my time must nearly be up. I'm going to get this prick if it's the last thing I do.

If only he knew.

Chapter 34

Three days to Anzac Day

Jack Ziegler was like a cat on a hot tin roof. He knew that he was being watched. The paranoia that was overtaking his mind told him so. The more he studied the faces at the café across the road the easier it was to figure out the times the two or three undercover police rotated themselves around. He would just have to stay truly alert, but he figured that was an easy ask if he just kept popping a few more pills. The murderous thoughts that crossed his mind were about all he was now concentrating on. The Establishment would pay.

That afternoon Ziegler had a funeral to do at his church, and he realised he had a perfect opportunity to get his pistol from its hiding place. It was one of his older parishioners that had died and when he had been contacted to do the service, he was told that the burial would be at the Melbourne General cemetery. A perfect chance. He busied himself around the parish grounds and to make it obvious that he didn't know about his 'shadowers' he even crossed the road and ordered a chai latte and a couple of cinnamon finger buns from the café and sat at one of the outside tables to eat them.

Deliberately looking at a now rather self-conscious undercover cop, he ate both of the buns very slowly, even stopping at the end to lick any excess cream off them. He had some preliminary funeral work to take care of so once he had finished, he threw the empty coffee container into a bin, rose and shook the excess crumbs off himself and sauntered back to the church yards. Once inside he looked at the clock and saw that he had a good two hours before the church service began. The parishioner was a very elderly man whom he had only met once and had forgotten his face even before he had started to shake the tissue-like trembling hand of the cancer ridden octogenarian. When the service started at two o'clock that afternoon, Ziegler would suddenly become bosom buddies with the deceased and wax lyrical about him in his eulogy. Hypocrisy at its best.

Many of the congregation approached Ziegler after the service and thanked him for looking after their friend or relative. Some even slipped him envelopes with cash in it for living expenses as a struggling parish pastor. Little did they know that the money would just go to feed his now insatiable pill popping habit.

After a short stay chatting outside the church, all the while standing with a large prayer book in his hand and a religious stole around his neck, Ziegler gently indicated to the closer relatives of the deceased that it was time for the cortege to make its way to the cemetery via the Le Pine funeral cars that were ready to transport them. Once they were herded in, he walked slowly, head down in what appeared to be solemn prayer in front of the slow-moving vehicles. As the cortege turned from the church onto the road, he walked to the passenger side of the hearse and got in. His plan had worked so far. Just as he turned to get in, he glanced at the coffee shop that was now basically next to the funeral procession and looked directly at two males who he noticed were the only people looking back at him. None of the other outside patrons had any interest in the funeral at all. The only car that was parked anywhere near the two men was a late model Ford Maverick utility and as he got into the hearse, Ziegler looked at the nearside mirror and watched the two go over to the big black utility. He would keep an eye out for that at the cemetery.

Ten minutes later when the cortege arrived at the gates of the cemetery in College Crescent, Ziegler got out to check the paperwork with the staff in the office and as he did so he had a perfect view of the half dozen cars that were in the cortege. As per most cars that were driving in a funeral procession, they had their headlights on so as to let other motorists know what they were doing. One car that was hanging back a little and had no lights on was the big black Ford utility.

Ziegler got back into the hearse with the appropriate paperwork and indicated to the driver to keep going along Entrance Avenue and then swing back around into First Avenue. His luck held because the gravediggers were waiting beside an open grave situated about three rows off First Avenue and about forty metres away from College Crescent. Well within striking distance of his real destination.

As he got out of the hearse again at the gravesite, he stood and waited next to the gravediggers and chatted with them. He only did this so he could see all the funeral cars pull up slowly. When he saw that the black utility had not joined at the rear of the cortege, he presumed it would be waiting in College Crescent for him on his departure. Another win.

The graveside service took only ten minutes or so to perform and then there was the normal scenario of shaking hands with the attendees before they all slowly drifted back to their vehicles and left. Ziegler walked over to the driver of the hearse and asked him to wait for him back at the cemetery office as he had a 'quick inspection of another parishioner's grave' to do nearby.

Picking his way quickly through an area of old broken graves and headstones, he got to the fence, ducked down, and looked around before placing his hand down alongside a crumbled grave top and pulling out the Smith and Wesson automatic that he had shot Billy McKay with. Removing his church stole from around his neck, he wrapped the plastic bag-covered-weapon in it and walked briskly back to the office. Minutes later he was in the passenger seat of the hearse and heading out the cemetery gates into College Crescent. Taking a quick look over his shoulder he spied the black utility pull out further back in the traffic and begin to follow the hearse. Once he got dropped off back at his church, Ziegler's cocky persona couldn't help itself as he sauntered across the road and ordered a double espresso to go. Crossing back across the road he walked slowly past the same black utility and into the front gate of the presbytery.

These guys couldn't track an elephant through snow, he thought as a satisfied grin crossed his face. Once inside he unwrapped the Smith and Wesson pistol from his stole and proceeded to clean it while his mind tried to work out where to get more 'recruits' to replace Rick Hawke, Ben Waite, and Billy McKay.

His delusional world kept turning.

Chapter 35

Two days to Anzac Day

The daily meeting at the Carlton police station was throwing up various situations and different people had varying opinions. One thing they all agreed on was that Anzac Day could not be ignored as a virtual D Day.

Johnny Petran's boys had reported back to group about the comings and goings of Jack Zeigler but basically there was no more real time information to tie him into anything. What they did believe was that since they had been 'dogging' him around the clock there had been no more incidents, but that could be just sheer coincidence. James Collins led the meeting.

"Max and Ethan have tracked down every single veteran who has or had a supposed grudge against the Army, Navy, and the Air Force. They have interviewed all possible candidates and to be honest they don't think any of them would have taken their grievances to the point of murder. They think this is down to someone with a real grudge against the system. Ziegler fits this bill. You agree Ethan?"

"Absolutely. This Anzac Day worries me though," Barnes said turning to all the others.

"What we need is some proof. How did your partner Tom get on with speaking to Ben Waite about what he knows about Ziegler when he was living at the church, Kate?" Tony Signorotto said.

"Short of beating it out of him there was nothing he would tell us. I think he has flash backs from his service days constantly although not as bad as when he first came to stay with us."

"How about we run with an idea of mine. Sorry to jump in here, but as I've said before, this is not going down on my patch without us throwing everything at it. Ethan, you are going to put a ring of steel around the Shrine in two days' time which is great.

I say we ramp that up right now if you can. Possible?"

Barnes looked at Collins who was nodding his head.

"We have the AFP troops. Max and I have been working side by side with some of the top brass at Victoria Barracks and I reckon they'll back us up at the Shrine with an SAS contingent from Campbell Barracks in Western Australia. They are over here at Swan Island down at Queenscliff doing a big training exercise. If anyone is going to try something at the Shrine, they'll have to be on top of their game to get around these guys. I'll get on to them right now."

"Great. James, as the Superintendent in charge of Metro, can you and the Vic police troops cover the Dawn Service and the Anzac March?"

"Already done. I've had the State Planning Unit in town write up the Operation Order for it. I'm parading everyone at headquarters at five a.m. on Anzac Day. I have over two hundred members covering the area. I'm taking Kate as my Staff Officer. What else, Tony?" Collins said, pleased to see his Senior Sergeant so focused on the job before him.

"Max and I are going to contact all the RSL clubs and Military establishments around Melbourne proper and give them a heads up. I don't think the clubs will be a target but I'm getting onto my contact at Parliament to make sure any politician that is laying a wreath anywhere has armed security with him."

"What about on Anzac Day, Tony. Where will you two be?" Collins said.

"Max can be liaison up at D24 overseeing any logistics problems. There will be a dedicated radio channel for the day, so I want him helping out up here. That okay with you, boss?"

"Fine by me, Max, but as I just asked, what will you be doing yourself. Where will you be?" a slightly confused James Collins asked.

"Looking after Carlton. I'll be available for anything that sticks it's head up as unusual or strange on the day." Signorotto said.

I'll be there when you do stick your head up, Ziegler. Signorotto smiled to himself with the thought.

What Tony Signorotto hadn't planned for was for Jack Ziegler's new regime of more pills and no sleep. He was ready to go into action sooner than they all thought.

Chapter 36

Anzac Day.

Johnny Petran was going to lead from the front for this Anzac Day threat. He had arranged to take over surveillance from one of his troops at one a.m. on Anzac Day outside Ziegler's church. After letting the other members of the Command group know this, he had gone to bed to get a few hours of sleep in the knowledge that Anzac Day for him was going to be a very long day. He'd only had his head down for about an hour when the shrill tone of his mobile phone rang on his bedside table. Picking it up quickly he heard the urgent voice of one of his team.

"Boss, he's on the move. Walked out just a few minutes ago with a backpack on. I'm following him up near the university at the moment."

As Petran put the phone onto loudspeaker he began to dress quickly.

"Just keep in the shadows. I'll try and head that way as quick as I can. Keep the calls coming and I'll let the others know," he said as he finished the call and quickly punched in Tony Signorototto's number.

"Tony, he's taken off on foot from the church. One of mine is dogging him. Thought you'd want to know."

Tony Signorotto leapt out of his own bed without disturbing his wife Susie, dressed in the bathroom and was heading down the stairs before she called out.

"What on earth are you doing? What's going on," she said urgently.

"Ziegler's on the prowl. Gotta go. Ring you later," he said grabbing his equipment belt which he had brought home. What was also on his belt, which technically should have been in the safe at Carlton, was his pistol. He never had any intention of getting into his uniform for Anzac Day but had not anticipated that Ziegler would kick off anywhere before about six o'clock that morning. That's when the Dawn Service started at the Shrine, but nothing was going to happen around Carlton before that. He looked at his watch as he threw his gear into his car and then realised, he didn't know where his quarry was or was even headed to. Grabbing his phone he rang Johnny Petran.

"Mate, I need real time updates. Get your guy on the radio and start up our own channel twenty-six. It's ours for the day so get him on it. I want to know where he is, and I don't want to sit here outside my house on my arse waiting." He disconnected the call, grabbed his portable radio off his equipment belt, and turned to the channel and waited for what seemed like an eternity till a call came up.

"Blue 815 to Senior Sergeant Signorotto," a reasonably calm voice said.

"Blue 810 here 815. Where is he now?"

"He's walked into the city through the Exhibition Gardens and is now walking up Victoria Parade towards the Fire Rescue headquarters."

"Roger that. Heading your way," Signorotto said, firing up his prize Ford Falcon GT and taking off with a screech of tyres. Through his earpiece he made a second radio call.

"Johnny, I want you to get onto the others and keep them up to speed."

"Okay Tony. Will do," came the staticky reply.

Signorotto was coming down Rathdowne Street when Ziegler's shadower came back on the radio.

"Passing outside Parliament House, boss."

"Okay, I'm just turning into Spring Street. I'll park the car and catch you up," Signorotto said as he grabbed his equipment belt, pulled to the kerb, and jumped out. He could see the pair of them on the other side of Spring Street, so he grabbed a jacket out of his car and threw it on over his firearm and walked quickly across the street. He caught up with the undercover police officer as they turned into Collins Street and started towards St Patrick's Cathedral.

"Where do you think he is going?" Signorotto said quietly.

"Don't know, but there are quite a lot of people up ahead near the Cathedral.

"Shit, of course," an upset Signorotto said in reply. "There's a five o'clock service on at St. Pats. It's on every year and a lot of people go there before going down to the Shrine for the Dawn Service. Christ, there are three doors to this place. Two at the side and the front of course and there's only bloody two of us."

Signorotto and the other member watched as Ziegler was swallowed up by the crowd going in the front doors.

"Can't just waltz in there wearing firearms," an exasperated Signorotto said as he got on the radio to get another member down to their location.

Signorotto had sent the undercover member to one of the side doors in case Ziegler came out that way, but he had an icy sensation go up and down his spine.

This guy is playing with us, I know he is.

Chapter 37

Jack Zeigler was no fool. He knew several times via surreptitious looks behind him as he walked towards St. Patrick's Cathedral that he was being followed. He just smiled to himself but was a bit surprised when he took a quick look as he went up the front stairs into the Catholic Cathedral that he saw the same undercover officer with another one who he had seen previously at the Carlton police station. He recognised Tony Signorotto immediately. He read his mind and could see his problem which Ziegler would exploit. Three doors, two cops.

Ziegler knew the layout of the Cathedral well, as he had been to many inter-denominational events held there. It was a cavernous building with a seating capacity of well over two thousand. For this annual Anzac Day service, he estimated there were about fifteen hundred present and that was without guessing the number of attendees that were offering up prayers at the seven chapels that were inside the Latin cross shaped home of worship to Melbourne's Catholic community. What he had to do once the service commenced was to get in a position at one of the side doors and see if either of the two police officers were lurking there. From the front of the cathedral, it was a much shorter walk to the Northern side door than the Southern door.

The service was not going to be more than thirty minutes, which gave all the worshippers a good thirty minutes to get to the Shrine of Remembrance if they wanted to for the official Dawn Service. Ziegler made his move from one of the side pews to the Southern door where he peered outside at the open garden area. There were a few late comers entering the door but there was no one outside that looked like they were waiting for him to make an exit. He took his chance and quickly stepped out into the shadows and made his way into Cathedral Place. He knew he had time to get to the South Yarra address of Simon Forbes. Thinking of various means of transport, he wasn't going to use his credit card to buy time on another e scooter or anything that could be tracked. Anzac Day was a public holiday and as such there were no fares to pay on public transport. Heading on foot quickly towards Collins Street he came across several bikes that were nosed into a bike rack near Spring Street. His luck was holding. One of them wasn't padlocked, so he pulled it out of the rack, jumped on it, and pedalled furiously down Spring Street and headed in the direction of the Melbourne Cricket Ground. There were plenty of pathways and such down there where he could head off to Punt Road and around a back way to his destination. As he rode, he could feel the weight of the pistol in his backpack banging heavily against his back. It was a long time since he had ridden a bicycle but there was no pain involved because he had pre-loaded on Ritalin to keep him going. Sleep was unnecessary. Revenge for 'his' men was paramount in his increasingly deranged mind.

***

"By the time more members came down, he'd gone." Tony Signorotto said with a totally frustrated sounding voice to James Collins over the phone. "We had to pick two doors to cover out of three and we lucked out. He could be anywhere. Remind me never to buy a Tattslotto ticket."

"The only place we know where he isn't is back at the church. I sent a uniform crew in and there is no-one there. There's not much else we can do until more information comes to light and I tend to agree with what you said before about playing with us. Let's not forget that this guy spent time in Iraq and for all we know he may have done other things except tend to his bloody flock. Just go back to Carlton and wait, Tony." Collins said.

"I take it the Dawn Service went off okay?" Signorotto said.

"Yes, it was business as usual except that we got asked a lot of questions about why there were so many Federal police doing our job. I'm not deploying them for the march. I've sent them back to their headquarters." Collins said.

"I thought Ethan said we had them for the day. What's

happened?" Signorotto replied quickly.

"Ethan is only an Inspector, Tony. Their hierarchy in Canberra got wind of them doing an unpaid operation for us and pulled the pin."

"Well, I suppose it was always going to come to this, but it's a bit like looking for a needle in a haystack and at the end of the day we have no proof that Ziegler has done anything except try and look after some Veterans, which reminds me that unfortunately we are going to have to lean on Ben Waite if anything else happens. He knows the connection between Ziegler and the gun that killed Billy Mckay and was used on Peter Galbraith. He just won't talk."

"Let's just try and get through today, eh?" a tired sounding Collins said before ending the call.

Chapter 38

It was after six thirty in the morning before Ziegler positioned himself behind Simon Forbes's BMW in the driveway of the Melbourne University Regiment's Colonel. Being April, it was getting quite cold, but Ziegler was shivering because of the Ritalin and lack of sleep, not the weather. He looked down at the loaded semi-automatic in his gloved hand and a calmness came over him. God had sent him to relieve the world of another war monger. This would absolutely bring headlines. Then he could go back to his church and carry on his recruiting quest. He had studied the website of the Melbourne University Regiment and had seen there was going to be a wreath laying ceremony there at nine o'clock that morning conducted by their Colonel-in-Chief. The timing was perfect.

Ziegler heard the door of Forbes's house shut and waited as the Colonel's boots stamped closer to his car. He actually spied the spit-polished footwear at the same time as he heard the electronic bip of the car doors unlocking. Ziegler pounced, grabbing the uniformed Colonel around the mouth at the same time as jamming the gun in his back and dragging him to the ground and out of sight. As a look of terror swept across Forbes's face, Ziegler swung the pistol upwards and then brought it down forcefully, cracking his victim across the side of the head and sending the terrified Forbes into unconsciousness. Knowing that Forbes was not married and that no-one said goodbye to him as he closed the front door, he didn't fear anyone rushing out of the house to see what the commotion was about. He quickly bundled the inert Forbes into the passenger side of the BMW and slid into the driver's seat before starting the powerful vehicle and heading slowly out of the drive.

"You've seen your last Anzac Day, Colonel," Ziegler said as he headed to his pre-planned destination.

"You'll be happy with where we are going, Simon," he said

talking to the still unconscious form strapped into the passenger seat belt sitting next to him. Any looks from people in other cars would be deflected by the dark window tinting that came as standard on the luxury vehicle.

It only took about fifteen minutes to drive to his destination. Ziegler knew that there would be nobody there as he parked behind the Scotch College rowing sheds on the Yarra river. Pulling a balaclava and a can of black spray paint from his backpack, he got out and walked up to each of the three CCTV cameras that were situated around the sheds and sprayed the lens each one making them useless. Getting back to the car, he opened the passenger door and dragged Forbes out by his hair. The hit to his head was now wearing off and the Colonel began to struggle violently as he tried to get up off the ground.

"No, you don't Colonel," Ziegler said as he kicked Forbes in the stomach causing the dishevelled soldier to double over and stay on the ground.

"Who are you? What have I done to you?" a defiant Forbes spat up at Ziegler.

"Oh, it's not you in particular I have a problem with, Simon. It's the War Machine Establishment you so proudly represent. You prime your troops up and lead them to believe when they go overseas that they are working for the great Australian military and that no matter what happens they will be looked after. You only have to look at what's happening with all the soldiers coming back and having medals stripped from them for so-called war crimes. What doesn't happen though is there is no blame laid on any of the military leaders. They just keep getting awards. The foot soldiers are thrown onto the scrap heap just to be forgotten. The government and the military just ignore them by handing out a paltry pension and a bit of medical assistance. You people are blind to their problems. I saw it because I served there. You are about to die for supporting the machine Simon so I can tell you this, I shot at the Defence Minister outside his home a while back and I also shot and killed a Veteran who I thought might stop me from my mission. I'm the one that shot up your beloved

University Regiment building. I didn't get any press out of these, so I have to take it to the next level and that means you have to die. Do you understand me?" the now raging Ziegler said inches away from the terrified face of Forbes.

"I've done nothing to you. My men don't serve overseas. They are just in reserve if the country ever needs them but governments for years have stated that they will never be sent overseas," a now almost hysterical Forbes said as he knelt in front of his executioner and felt the barrel of Ziegler's pistol press against his forehead.

"You should have stuck to making money Simon Forbes. You are one of those elite types. One of the privileged few. A good little Public-School boy from Scotch College. Did you ever row for your school down here, Simon," he said taking the gun from Forbes's head and waving it around in the direction of the sheds and river.

"No, no. I didn't," Forbes said with a terrified voice in between loud sobs.

"I didn't think you did, Simon. I would say that you would have been an upstanding member of the Scotch College cadets. Marching around like a chocolate soldier with your old rifle on your shoulder and just waiting to go to Puckapunyal Army base every year to play war games. Then after graduation you went off to good old Melbourne University to study commerce or such and continue your obsession with the uniform by joining the Melbourne University Regiment and having pass-the-port nights at your fancy dinners while the real soldiers were face down in sand in Afghanistan and Iraq being shot at. Am I right?"

"Can pick your sort a mile away. You've probably never looked down the business end of a firearm, have you? Well, this time you are going to," Ziegler said as he pulled back the slide on the Smith and Wesson firearm thus pulling one of the fifteen rounds into the barrel. He placed the gun back against the sweating forehead of his kneeling and shaking captive.

"Stop shaking and accept your fate, you war monger. Look up."

The tear-stained face of Simon Forbes slowly raised itself so his eyes were in line with the barrel of the pistol.

"Why me. I haven't ...."

The bullet entered between his eyes and exploded out the back of his head, taking a large piece of his skull and most of his brain and splattered it all against the concrete wall of the boat shed. Forbes's body slumped backwards to the ground.

Ziegler smiled to himself as he watched a cascade of blood pump from the remaining section of Forbes's head down onto the Colonel's insignia of his khaki uniform.

Ziegler left the body where it was. He was only concerned about any incriminating DNA that may be on the vehicle now. Taking a small plastic container of petrol from his backpack together with a rag, he soaked it with petrol then removed the fuel cap from the BMW. After stuffing the rag into the fuel filler area, he poured the rest of the patrol over the side of the car.

Taking a change of shirt and jeans from the same backpack, he was ready to go. As he walked away, he removed a box of matches from his pack, struck one and flicked it towards the luxury car. The trailing fuel rag caught immediately and trailed up to and then inside the fuel filler. An almighty whoosh then erupted skywards before engulfing the car in flame.

Ziegler walked away from the scene with his backpack over his shoulder. Now it was time for his next encore as he took out his burner phone and opened the 'Magic Voice Changer' application ready to begin another game with the police, but not until he was within a short distance of home.

Chapter 39

Tony Signorotto had only been back at Carlton for a short while but decided to check up on the various RSL's and military places to see if there had been any problems. The main Anzac Day march had only been going about one hour and so far, there hadn't been any issues.

He had rung around most of the RSL's when one of the members downstairs came up from the watch house area.

"Boss, there's a Lieutenant Clunes on the phone for you. Thinks there's something you may want to know."

"Where's he from?" Signorotto replied tiredly thinking that his day could only get worse.

It was about to.

"Melbourne University Regiment," the young member replied.

A cold shiver went through Signorotto as he told the member to put the call through.

"Senior Sergeant Signorotto here Lieutenant. How can I help?"

"We were told to contact you if anything strange had happened today," Clunes said.

'What do you mean? What's happened?" a nervous Signorotto replied.

"Well, we were meant to hold a wreath laying ceremony this morning at nine o'clock, but the strange thing is that the Colonel of the Regiment hasn't shown up. He was meant to be running the service, but as I said, he hasn't shown, and we can't get him on his phone. I ran the service, but he still hasn't fronted."

Signorotto's body tingled with fear. "What's his name and where does he live?"

"Colonel Simon Forbes. He lives over South Yarra way."

"Has he ever been late before for any reason?"

"Never. He prides himself on being early by an hour or so. It's really out of character for him. Since the Regiment building was shot at a while ago, he has been here even more. I thought when I turned up at eight that he would have already been here, but the gates were locked."

"Give me his phone number and details of his car. Is he married?"

"No, he's not married. No kids. It's really strange."

After getting all the details he could from Clunes, he assured him he would be back in contact as soon as he could. Once he had finished his call, he was about to re-dial the desk phone when it rang.

"Signorotto here. Who's this?"

There was a moment of silence, and just before Signorotto went to speak again, a slight metallic buzzing sound came over the phone before what sounded like a computer-generated voice could be heard.

"Who's this?" Signorotto said with nervous voice that was now totally waiting for an answer.

"Scotch College rowing sheds on the Yarra. The chocolate soldier has now melted, but there are more at Melbourne Central I'm sure," the unidentifiable computer sounding voice said before the metallic sound of screeching laughter erupted over the phone causing Signorotto to hold the phone well away from his ear. When he again put the phone to his ear, he heard two shots being fired in rapid succession. "Lots of fake soldiers here at Melbourne Central."

"Wait, wait. What are you saying?" Signorotto said as he scribbled down the words TRACE THIS CALL and ran down the stairs handing the note to Kate McLaren. "I cannot...." The call ended with no time to trace it.

"Kate, drop everything and get a crew to Melbourne Central. I'll get you back up. Shots have been fired."

"I'll have to take the two away from keeping a watch for Ziegler. There's no one else. They are all on the Anzac March down St. Kilda Road and the van and the only traffic car are tied up at a fatal in Collingwood."

"Do it. I'll get onto D24 and Collins. It was a computer-controlled voice, and he talked about the Scotch College rowing sheds and something about a melted chocolate soldier."

One of the watch house Senior Constables spun around and spoke.

"Boss, did it say something about a chocolate soldier?"

"Signorotto was rubbing his face in total confusion as he vaguely replied. "Yeah, why. What are you going on about?"

"Boss, a chocolate soldier is one who is in the Army Reserve. Not a regular soldier. The saying is that we melt under heat. I'm in Army Reserve Military Police. Everyone who is in the Reserve is jokingly referred to as that. Everyone from Privates up to Colonels."

Signorotto's face turned white.

"No, no. It couldn't be. No, no," he said with a terrified look on his face.

Chapter 40

Tony Signorotto knew that D24 didn't have a choice in calling in the crew that was sitting off Ziegler's church in North Carlton. After all, he made the call that shots had been fired so there was nothing else for it. Most of the police around the CBD were tied up with the Anzac Day march. Nothing else for it. He had even sent Kate McLaren and the counter crew off in a car, so it was up to him to man the police station by himself.

Jack Ziegler knew that the police department would have to take this job as a priority. Tony Signorotto would have been on the radio to D24 immediately, so he had positioned himself right at the end of one of the railway platforms and after about two minutes had quietly jumped down over the end into the darkness where he let off two shots from his Smith and Wesson, climbed back up quickly after stuffing the gun into his backpack, lowered his baseball cap and walked back along the platform. He could see the shots had caused panic on the crowded platform with people running towards the escalators trying to escape what they probably thought was a mass shooting. He helped the panic along by screaming that there was a man with a gun and pointing in the direction of where he had been.

By the time he had squeezed and pushed his way out onto Swanston Street he could hear sirens coming from the direction of Carlton and saw a few police officers running across from the State Library. Pushing his collar up and cap down, he rushed up to a north bound tram and climbed aboard just as it was about to head back up towards the university area.

He got off half way along Swanston Street and made his way through the many back alleyways and small streets that made up the fabric of Carlton until he was within sight of not only his church but also of the café where he knew the undercover police members had been constantly keeping track of him. Being Anzac Day and a public holiday, it was closed, so he walked slowly around the area of the church and the parish house. There was no-one in sight. Entering quickly, he leant against the inside of the door of the rectory and breathed a sigh of relief. Next was the gun.

Ziegler was so sure that God had sent him on this mission of death and retribution that he had no qualms about taking the murder weapon, entering the empty church, and putting it in one place where only he had access to. The Tabernacle on the altar. To have an instrument of death next to the symbol of peace being the consecrated hosts never crossed his mind.

He returned to the parish house, sat down and started to watch the remainder of the Anzac Day march on television and found himself in almost childlike delight when the coverage crossed to a news bulletin outside Melbourne Central station where he could see hundreds of people being kept away while heavily armed police began to descend down onto the platforms.

"You are no match for me, Signorotto," Ziegler said to himself as he reached for a vial containing Ritalin tablets. "God is on my side."

Chapter 41

"If this person wanted publicity, then he sure as hell has got it," an angry Assistant Commissioner for Crime said to those he had summoned to his office at Police headquarters the day after Anzac Day. As well as James Collins, Tony Signorotto and Max Tyler, there were two Detective Sergeants from the Homicide Squad. It did not bode well for the future of the small Carlton task force.

"This is now in the public domain. A murder, or actually an execution, of a member of the Army Reserve on Anzac Day has hit the headlines. From the looks of it, Colonel Simon Forbes was abducted as he went to his car to go to the service at the Melbourne University Regiment. Not only didn't he get there but he ended up being shot to death down by the Scotch College boatsheds. The perpetrator of this and obviously another murder and the shooting up of an Army Reserve establishment has got the whole city on edge. If you add in what was really a botched attempt on the life of the Federal Veteran Affairs Minister, Mr. Galbraith we have an obvious serial killer of military personnel on our hands. So obvious that I take the blame for not handing over this messy business to the Homicide Squad much earlier. I have tendered my resignation to the Chief Commissioner because as I said, I thought we could get this killer without getting headlines. I was wrong. These cases are now the property of these two Detective Sergeants from Homicide," he said indicating the two new faces in the room. Tony Signorotto could not help but speak up.

"Sir, I know and the rest of those who have worked this know that Jack Ziegler is the person responsible. He is as cunning as a shit-house rat and has been able to out manoeuvre us. We just can't get any proof that he has done what we all know he has done. Can we at least stay involved with the Homicide boys here?"

"No. This needs fresh eyes. Give everything you have to them and then go back to work at Carlton, or as in your case, Mr. Collins, to your new posting as Superintendent of the Police Academy. Don't blame me because I will be paying the biggest price of all, which is my job. The Chief has had the State Government come down on him through the Police Minister like a ton of bricks and you all know the saying," he said looking around before continuing. "When the shit starts flowing down hill, don't live in the valley. Well, it looks like we have all been caught on this one. Inspector Ethan Barnes from the Feds will be demoted as well and I have to say that Command is looking at placing a new Senior Sergeant in charge at Carlton. With a state election in six months' time, the last thing the government of the day wants is for the public to think its police force has lost its ability to solve major crime."

Silence engulfed the room as a few sets of feet shuffled below the conference table. James Collins went to speak.

"Sir, it's not that...." He said before being cut off by the Assistant Commissioner.

"It's nothing personal, James. As I stated, I will not survive this and others here will take a hit, but myself, you and Tony are the leaders of this so we will bear the brunt of it. Please stay here and give all your current information to these detectives," he said sweeping his hand to one side as the two Homicide detectives stepped away from the table and he exited the room.

James Collins stepped quietly over to Tony Signorotto who sat with a stunned look on his face.

"They'll put me on enforced leave, James what's the bet?" a quiet Signorotto said.

"In hindsight, Tony, we should have cast our net wider than just Carlton. That's my fault," Collins said in reply.

"We know Ziegler is our man, but if these guys from Homicide start by putting all the rocks back down and then looking back under them again, it will just give him confidence to do something else. We have to keep going on him," Signorotto said with a lost sounding voice.

"Mate, from next week, I will be hung out to dry checking on recruits out at the Academy at Glen Waverley. I won't be able to do anything at all. Max will have to come back to headquarters and work day-to-day crime cases. You will have to see if they shove you to one side or put Kate up in charge. If you can stay, that is good. Just keep your head down. He never said they were sending you off on leave, and if they want to, it will take a few weeks of paperwork and manoeuvring before they can make you. Have the Police Association on the end of the phone twenty-four-seven. Just stall for time if you have to."

"What are you getting at, James? If I'm out, then I'm out," Signorotto replied.

"Mate, you live and breathe Carlton. It runs through your blood. You've grown up there and as you said, we both know who has done this shit. It's Ziegler. And where does he live? He lives on your patch, and he is successfully ending careers here. Don't let him do it. Fuck the Chief's office. Get Max aside and nail this bloke. Let Kate in on it and she will run Carlton while you just go after him. You just have to find proof and the way to get that is to get Ben Waite on side. We know he saw Ziegler do something on the night Billy McKay was killed. You have to get it out of him. That gun is the best piece of evidence you can find. Just concentrate on that. It will take these Homicide boys a few weeks of raking over the stuff that we have all collected on Ziegler before they dot their I's and cross their T's. Use the time," Collins said with passion.

"I'll be done after this, mate. I've had enough. If I'm getting the chop, I'll go out my way," Signorotto said with a glint in his eye before stepping over to give some details to the new case detectives.

"That's the Tony Signorotto I've come to know," Collins said.

Chapter 42

Jack Ziegler found out quickly that Tony Signorotto was not going away. Days after he had executed Simon Forbes, he was about to step into the pulpit of his church for the regular Sunday service when he heard someone cough very close to his back as he put one hand on the pulpit handrail. Turning slightly to see why someone was so close, his eyes widened upon seeing the swarthy plain-clothed figure of the Senior Sergeant. Before he could speak, Signorotto did.

"I'm going to live in your dreams, Jack. You are going to see me every which way you turn," Signorotto whispered so that no members of the very small congregation overhead him.

"What are you talking about? Get away from me," a clearly shaken Ziegler said nervously.

"Let's talk after church, eh Jack?" Signorotto said stepping past the Minister whilst not moving his eyes from him as he proceeded to sit in a pew a few rows from the front.

Ziegler proceeded to climb up the few steps of the pulpit. His next ten minutes or so giving a sermon to his flock was spent nervously looking down at the smiling Senior Sergeant who never took his eyes off him. By the time he had finished his talk, Ziegler couldn't remember what he had even spoken about. His sermon notes were a pulpy mess in his hand, caused by the sweat that was coursing over his body. The one thing he did notice was that members of his congregation were turning to each other with puzzled looks on their faces.

When the service was finally over, Ziegler placed himself just outside the front door of the church as he usually did after the day's worship to say hello to his congregation. The numbers at his church were dropping significantly due to his continuous anti-government rants that clearly had begun to not only upset members of his church but also causing a group of them to approach their Bishop with their concerns about Ziegler's suitability to remain their pastor. Very few of them stopped to chat. One exception was Tony Signorotto who waited till there were only the two of them remaining.

"I will bring you down, Ziegler. I will never go away until I have the proof to put you away. You will see me here at your church, you will see me at the supermarket, on your walks and wherever else you go. I have time. I have lots of time," Signorotto said with a voice that sounded as though it would cut through steel.

Getting a little bit of confidence back, Ziegler began to speak.

"And just what is it that you think I have done?"

"Oh, I don't think it, I know it. You murdered Billy McKay probably because he saw you shoot up the Army barracks. You shouldn't have left him there, Jack. That was a mistake. Too obvious a connection. Then there is where it all started back with Peter Galbraith. You have a real hatred of all military, don't you?"

"You have no evidence of me doing anything wrong, Signorotto. If you did, we wouldn't be standing here with you throwing false accusations around. I am going to report you for harassment."

"I have been in your church and listened a while ago to your rants about the Government and the military in particular. You are obsessed with returning veterans and their treatment. We have looked into your past record as a military religious and the way you had to leave Iraq. We know all about you. If you think we cannot join the dots on all the military things that have happened around Carlton and even down at the boatsheds then you are a fool, Jack. Don't think some pathetic threat to report me will get you anywhere. I'm on extended leave right now and, you know what, I don't like gardening much. I prefer to walk the streets of Carlton. My Carlton you low life piece of shit. Make all the phone calls you want. I'll give you the phone number of my Superintendent even. You can talk to the man himself who runs this area and see if you do any good. How does that sound?"

Trying to call Signorotto's bluff, Ziegler decided to go on the offensive.

"Give me his name, and his phone number right now. I demand it!"

Tony Signorotto stood opposite Ziegler as he called out his Superintendent's name and phone number.

"Superintendent James Collins. Work mobile 0433 121 799."

"I will be ringing him in a minute. Now get out of my sight and stop harassing me," Ziegler said stepping around Signorotto and walking towards his house.

First step to setting you up, Ziegler.

Chapter 43

"Mr. Ziegler, is that how I should address you?" James Collins said with an apologetic tone.

"It's Reverend Ziegler, Superintendent."

"My apologies, Reverend. If what you say is correct, and I have no doubt that you may be, I will be having severe words with Senior Sergeant Signorotto about his behaviour. He has been under a lot of stress recently along with other members due to the shootings and murders that have happened in the Carlton district. What did he say exactly?" Collins asked into his mobile phone as he sat in his private car next to Tony Signorotto just three streets from Ziegler's Church of the Uniting Spirit in Palmerston Street.

"He accused me of murdering Billy McKay amongst other things." Ziegler ranted into his phone.

"Well, that is not on, Mr. Ziegler. There is nowhere enough proof that you had anything to do with poor Billy's death. My Task Force has been investigating that for a while now and we are short of evidence in regard to that point. We have quite a few leads to go on regarding that and the death of the Army Reserve officer Simon Forbes on Anzac Day, but we have a long way to go yet," Collins said as he faced Signorotto who was sitting opposite in the passenger seat. Collins had the car running and the car's speaker on so Signorotto could hear every word of the conversation.

"I hope you don't think I had anything to do with Colonel Forbes's death," Ziegler said immediately with a worried tone. "I was at home. Nowhere near the Scotch College rowing sheds. This is harassment of the highest order. You back off now and get that attack dog of yours to do the same before I call in my solicitor do you hear?"

"Don't worry Mr. Ziegler, I will..."

"It's Reverend Ziegler, Superintendent," came the enraged

voice over the phone.

"Sorry Mr Ziegler. My fault," Collins said with a smile towards Signorotto. "As I was going to say. I'll have a word to him, but I can't until he comes back from his leave in a few weeks."

"He obviously hasn't gone anywhere because he was in my church an hour ago accusing me of murder. Get onto him and tell him to back off and stay away from my church. Do you understand, Superintendent?"

"Absolutely Mr, sorry Pastor. However, even if I saw him in the street now, I can't mention any work-related items because he is on leave. Strict rules of the department you must understand. I would be in hot water also if I told him to stay away from your church. You know what it's like with religious rights and such. I will definitely sit him down for a talk when he returns, but for now you'll just have to be satisfied that you've told me, Mr. Ziegler."

Collins smiled as Ziegler screamed the word 'Reverend' out loud and ended the call.

"I think we may have Jack Ziegler a tad concerned, don't you, mate?" Collins said to a smiling Signorotto.

"I think we keep our little game in-house for the moment. You, me Max and Kate," Signorotto said from the passenger seat.

"We'll get him. Just from that call alone he has tripped up badly. First off, neither I nor the papers put Simon Forbes in as a Colonel and secondly, neither I nor the papers mentioned it was outside the Scotch College rowing sheds. The only place that was mentioned in the papers was that he was found down by the river. Scotch College was never mentioned at all," Collins said with a sly smile on his face.

"We'll keep loading the gun, James. Let him pull the trigger," a smiling Signorotto said. "In the meantime, we have no choice but to try and find out what Ben Waite really knows. This is much bigger than just him now."

Chapter 44

Jack Zeigler thought he had picked a good night as he huddled in the caravan doling out soup and sandwiches to the underprivileged in Elizabeth Street in the heart of the CBD. The rain came in intermittent heavy showers and when they stopped you realised how cold it was.

Taking a break after a few hours, he wandered amongst the huddles that lay in the shop doorways or on the footpath. There were more than the normal numbers sleeping rough that night. Ziegler felt empathy for them, but he was only targeting one particular type. He wanted a returned service person. Walking towards Flinders Lane he spied a man in what he believed to be his late thirties. It was hard to tell with the covering of clothes and general grime that most were layered in. He approached the male who stared back at him with an angry look.

"Hello my friend. I'm Reverend Jack Ziegler from the Uniting Church in Carlton..."

"What the fuck are you doing here then, eh?" the man said raising himself up to where he stared down on Ziegler. "You trying to convert me or something?"

"No, no. Not at all," Ziegler replied nervously realising he was talking to a quite agitated person. "I'm here with the food van which gives out food and blankets to those in need. Just checking that you are doing okay tonight," he said with a note of sympathy to his voice. The big man stepped back a little before he spoke.

"Yeah, I'm doing okay for the moment. Thought you were going to bible bash me or something."

"Never do that. It's just a welfare chat really," Ziegler replied. "If I may ask though, you're a big fella and look as though you could take care of yourself. How did you end up in this position? Domestic problems or did you lose your job in these bad times?"

"Just had enough of the system. It's supposed to look after you but sometimes you need more than a handout from the bloody Federal government. They toss you aside when you come back. Give this country service and they think they can fob you off with money."

Ziegler's mind went into overdrive. He put out his arm to shake hands.

"As I said. Jack Ziegler is my name. Can I get yours?"

An outstretched hand came slowly in return. "Mick Gray."

"You mentioned the Federal Government Mick. What did you do to be on their books?" Ziegler laughed falsely.

"Two tours with the Paras in Iraq. One should have been enough, but they said I was fine to go back again. I bloody wasn't."

"Know the feeling Mick. I was a pastor over there too. Come back here and lucky enough to be given the church up in Carlton to see me through a lot of bad shit memories. Are you staying anywhere besides these luxurious Melbourne City Council footpaths?" Ziegler said with a grin on his face.

"Been around here and was offered council digs up at their place in North Melbourne but I don't like living in a place where there is no lock on the door and a lot of druggies hanging around wanting to pinch things from you, if you get what I mean," Gray said.

"I know where you are coming from, Mick. I've dealt a fair bit with returned veterans around here. How about coming over to the caravan and we can have a chat? See if we can help each other out a bit. I'd say your opinion of government assistance is about the same as mine. Just being dumped out of one of the Services doesn't fix the problems for a lot of us," Ziegler said as he slowly walked a couple of steps away. Gray knelt down and picked up his old swag and a few clothes and fell in step behind him until they had got back around the corner. Ziegler talked as they walked.

"Where abouts were you with the Paras?"

"All over the place. Jumped in, did the job, and got out. Never knew where I was half the time. Think that's why I'm finding it hard to settle back down in one spot."

Back at the van, Ziegler made room for Gray under the big side awning that covered the stacks of produce that had been donated by various restaurants. It was all good food that was nearing its expiry date. Something that they didn't have to bother about at the caravan as it was gratefully given and devoured very quickly.

"You know Mick, why should someone like you, who has served his country so well have to suffer. Yes, they give you a pension but they should be trying to re-employ you and get you on your own two feet, not drip feeding with a few dollars and thinking that's all you need," Ziegler said with a slightly angry voice as he handed Gray a cup of coffee and a packet of sandwiches.

"We get psych help and medical help but what we need are training courses to get us back into the work force. The hardest thing of all is getting back to work. You can't get anywhere without references, and the government doesn't supply those. Some of their people at Vet Affairs just think everything will fall into place. People don't see that we come back messed up."

"That's right. Excuse the language from a Minister but they are fucking stupid. I have tried to shake things up both here and with those fools in Canberra, but I think what we need is some direct action. You know, get right in their faces. Don't want to get violent but we have to do what is necessary for guys like you. Tell you what, would you be interested in some free room and board up at my church? I'm trying to get a group of returned Vets together so we can sort of 'rise up against the machine' if you get my drift. Had a few of the guys come and stay, but one was always drugged and the other just up and left for some shitty job in a café. I'd like to see a few of us force the hand of the Federal Government, no matter what it takes. You've been deserted in a lot of ways Mick and it's not bloody right. Let's start to make an impact," Ziegler said raising his voice. Mick Gray looked at him and took a step backwards.

"You take this personally, don't you?" Gray said.

"I was trying to help over there in Kandahar, and they shut me down and shipped me back. Said I was a bad influence on the troops. It was all rubbish. They were just trying to justify sending boys to their death. This government has to be taken down. Start with the Defence people in Canberra and keep going with the fools that run the Armed Forces. I am absolutely committed to making headlines. Anyway, you want a roof over your head?"

Mick Gray looked sheepishly at Ziegler before he spoke.

"Could do with a sleep out from under the stars. I don't mind telling you it's nice to meet a person who understands the real plight of Vets. I'm sick of this country trying to fob us off."

"That's great Mick. I have a couple more hours here but if you want to make your way up to the Uniting Spirit church in Palmerston St, North Carlton, I'll see you there," Ziegler said with a big smile on his face.

Gray picked up his gear and wandered back to Flinders Lane where he walked towards Collins Street. Stopping and checking behind him he then walked west along Collins Street. As he walked past an old Ford Falcon, the passenger side front door swung open. Gray threw his gear into the back seat of the car and climbed in before speaking to the driver.

"Sitting off that food van finally paid off, eh boss?"

"Love your work Mr. Gray," Tony Signorotto said.

Chapter 45

Over a coffee two mornings later, Mick Gray' began to wean information from Jack Ziegler.

"You've told me you were a chaplain when you served, but what has really got you so riled up about the way veterans are being treated. We do get a reasonable deal when we get out. After all, we put our hands up to go overseas," the veteran police officer who had taken leave to help Tony Signorotto to bring Ziegler down said.

James Collins, Signorotto and the veteran whose real name was Sergeant Brian Gold and also a returned serviceman from the Iraq war, knew they would have to do all this without any real help as Collins and Signorotto had been told to leave any investigation to the Homicide squad. So far, the investigation by the elite squad had not got anywhere.

"I suppose it's just the way the generals and the army hierarchy leave all the dirty work to the troops themselves while they sit back here and wine and dine at places like the Melbourne Club and the Atheneum Club. A lot more should be done to equalise the ranks and give more of the ground troops the right to call the shots," Ziegler said in reply.

Gold took a chance with his next statement.

"You sound like a member of the Russian military or something. No matter what you think, there must be a rank structure, so the machine works effectively whether you like it or not. You didn't try and subvert the cause over there did you because that would be classified as treason," Gold said hoping to get under Ziegler's skin.

Gold had hit a nerve. Ziegler stood from the table, spilling his cup of coffee over his breakfast as he began to shout.

"How dare you. I'm as loyal as the next soldier. These fucking army top dogs have no idea what they are doing. I got sent home because I challenged them and their ways. They should all be put up against a wall and shot as far as I'm concerned," a ranting Ziegler shouted before snapping back to almost normality in front of the well-composed Gold. What he didn't know was that Gold was recording every word that was spoken on a mini recorder he had in the top pocket of his old, tattered shirt that he was wearing.

"Who are you talking about when you say they should be killed? Not the ones in uniform surely. Even the Top Brass are only carrying out the wishes of the government of the day," a prodding Gold said.

Ziegler went very quiet before he spoke again.

"Do you want to get some other veterans together here at my church? We could then really challenge the authoritarian lackeys," Ziegler said with what Gold could see was a faraway look in his eyes.

"How would we do that? Running up and down through the city will just piss people off. So will marching on places like the Department of Veteran Affairs," Gold said hoping for some information. What he got for a reply was the same as his name-Gold!

Ziegler's eyes narrowed and seemed to take on a Machiavellian appearance.

"I have unfinished business with the bastard that is the head of that mob."

Gold knew it was a risk, but he had to get as much on his recorder as he could. For all he knew, Ziegler might snap and throw him out or just shut up completely. He had only been at the church a couple of days, and he had already seen Ziegler throw tablets down his throat like there was no tomorrow. He had taken a chance the night before and looked at the packaging of them. Some he didn't know but he saw that Ziegler was taking large doses of Ritalin. It all equated with his aggressive outbursts such as what had happened just before.

"Who are we talking about? You mean the guy that is in charge of the Victorian DVA?"

Ziegler's eyes darted towards Gold as his mouth split into a malicious grin.

"I don't deal with minions. I'm talking about that bastard Peter Galbraith. We have unfinished business. Don't start me on him. He is the person responsible for the treatment of veterans, and he doesn't do anywhere near enough for them. All he does is take in a huge pay packet every week. He'll wait though. God will get him," he said, turning away to stare into the distance.

Gold quickly felt the tiny recorder in his shirt pocket. To his relief, it was still recording. He decided to change the conversation.

"Fair enough. What's on your agenda for today? Church stuff?"

"I don't write sermons anymore. Just get up and talk from the heart. Usually, to do with the injustices that people are putting up with all the time. People are harassed by councils, police, you name it. We all have to stand up and be counted, Mick. I have to go back to the food van tonight. How about you come along? If there are any veterans around, we may be able to add to our little compound here. Build it all up again. Last three were all over the place."

"If you don't mind me asking, what happened. Why didn't they stay? After all, you've been good enough to help me out the last couple of days," Gold said.

"One decided to get away and get a job in a café. Another got himself shot one night when he wandered away. Hopeless drug addict though. I couldn't help him. The third guy got frightened by the police who thought I was involved in the tragedy. We were going along okay and then I was finding myself having to start all over. We need a strong group where we can do things together. Stick together like we did in the desert."

"Do what sort of things?" Gold pressed.

"Put things right again, Mick. Put things right. We'll show 'em," Ziegler said quietly whilst looking around as if there were people listening in the otherwise empty room.

The lift doesn't go to the top floor with this nutter, Gold thought.

Chapter 46

Tony Signorotto was just pulling into his driveway when his mobile phone rang. Looking at the number he thought it was just a cold-caller or such so he let it ring through. He was surprised when he got inside his house that there was an actual voice mail message left. Grabbing a cold drink from the fridge he sat down and played the message. He never took a sip of his drink as he placed it quickly on the coffee table and re-dialled the number that was showing. As it connected, he didn't have a chance to speak before the male on the other end took over.

"Tony, I'm not giving you my name because if this turns to shit then you can honestly say you didn't know who rang you, okay?"

"Whatever. The voicemail said you had some interesting news about the shooting of Colonel Simon Forbes. Why are you ringing me and how did you get my phone number?" an intrigued Signorotto asked.

"Nothing to concern yourself about, Tony. Just take it in that I may have been one of those Homicide detectives that was at the briefing when you and James Collins got the heave-ho from anything to do with Jack Ziegler and I think it was pretty wrong that both of you got put off the case. In saying that, I'll give you some news and this will be the last phone call you receive from me. Understand?"

"Understood. What's the information?"

"So far except for one thing, we haven't been able to get any closer to Ziegler. This piece of information is for you and you only. I know you'll probably share it with Collins and maybe even Max Tyler, but you never got this from me. We have lifted prints off the back of Forbes's car that was found at the rowing sheds."

Signorotto sat bolt upright in his chair and waited.

"I'm a bit like you when it comes to Ziegler," the voice said. "I wouldn't trust him an inch. I ran the prints through the Defence Force database and guess what. They are a match for the good Reverend Jack Ziegler. Thought you'd like to know. I've also got some insiders who have told me you are running a bit of an off the grid campaign in regard to Ziegler."

"First things first. That's great about the prints, and yes, a couple of us were pretty pissed off about being taken off his case so we decided to run it whilst on leave. You have an objection to us trying to pin this scumbag to the wall? Some of us are absolutely convinced he is behind everything. You agree?"

"I have to play the official line, Tony, but if I was in your position I would wear him as tight as a shadow. He is a nasty piece of work. I'll keep reporting back to Command but besides the prints we are getting nowhere. We need more than that. A lot more. We are going to need to question Ben Waite as he was the last veteran staying at that church. In saying that you may want to speak to him first. I don't know if he saw or knows anything about the night Billy McKay died but we have to keep looking under all the rocks."

"Thanks for the info. I might give him another visit before you guys do. I think he'd really clam up if he saw the Hommies walk up his path."

"A pleasure doing business with you, Tony. At the end of the day, we all have the same goal in mind," the detective signed off with.

Signorotto immediately rang James Collins and relayed the information from the 'anonymous' caller.

"What we really want is that gun, Tony. The prints are great, but that slippery prick could make up anything about it. Could even say that he knew Forbes through some military connection. It's good, but we want that piece of hardware. Do you think Brian Gold could have a good look around inside the church house?"

"I'll try and get hold of him. He's due to meet me at Dom's tomorrow so I'll see if he can."

"I'd be surprised if he's got rid of it. If we are correct, it's tied to two murders, one attempted murder and the shooting up of the MUR barracks, so he's had it a while now and I've been thinking about it a lot. We've been through the church house once. This guy's no idiot. He'd have trouble trying to get another piece as you are keeping a pretty close eye on him. The only other place is the church itself. See if Gold can offer some cleaning service for the cost of his lodgings and sweep the aisles or something. That way he can have a good look around when Ziegler's not there," Collins said.

"See how we go. I'm due to sit in on a church service again this Sunday to keep letting him see that his plea to you about me leaving him alone has fallen on deaf ears. I want to keep eyeballing him, so he knows we aren't about to give up. Might even see if Rick Hawke is on a day off. That would really put the wind up him as he reaches the height of his sermon."

Chapter 47

Tony sat at the back of Dom's restaurant and was just finishing his first long black when Brian Gold walked in and sat beside him. Dom Santino never asked questions of his old friend Tony Signorotto so even though he had never seen Gold before it was obvious that this was a business meeting, and the only sort of business that Tony Signorotto conducted in the Lygon Street restaurant was police business. Enough said.

"Coffee sir?" Dom asked in a way that avoided Tony's eyes so that he didn't have to be introduced to the new customer.

"Long black thanks," Gold replied.

Coppers coffee, thought Dom as he quickly went towards the kitchen.

"Brian, are you getting anywhere with Ziegler?" Tony asked.

"Well, I can tell you this much. He hates all governments with a passion and one thing he did let slip is that he has unfinished business with Peter Galbraith."

"Wow. That could only mean one thing and that is the fact that the shooter missed Galbraith outside his home. We've also been able to tie him to a set of prints on the back of Colonel Simon Forbes's car, so that's one attempted murder and one cold blooded execution plus the shells that were found after the murder of Billy McKay. All military people. What we need though is a direct link to the gun that was used in both. I don't think he has ditched it because he has used it three times and he could have gotten rid of it after the first."

"You know, I think there would be one place where you could hide something and no-one would ever think to search," Gold said.

"I've been thinking the same thing. His church. The only trouble is that we have already searched his house next to it and come up with nothing. If we go for a search warrant on the church it would have to go all the way to the top due to the religious connection. What's the chances of you having a poke around?" Signorotto said as a sly smile crossed his face.

"Can't see why not. It's about time I offered to do some jobs around the place to earn my keep so I might even suggest that I can sweep the church also. I had a quick peep in there the other day and there were elderly parishioner doing the sweeping and other things. I pretended to be just a passer-by and asked how come they were doing the upkeep. One guy mumbled something and tried to hush up one of the ladies who was putting flowers into a vase. She stated straight away that the whole place was becoming a shambles and that the only time Ziegler spent in the church was when he ranted and raved from the pulpit. She did not look happy and I thought that both of them were a bit afraid of the good Minister."

"That would be great, Brian. In the meantime I'm going to visit my fellow Senior Sergeant, Kate McLaren and her husband Tom who just happens to have one of Ziegler's escapees as a boarder. I'm taking an ex-army mate of his along who I need him to listen to, Rick Hawke."

Chapter 48

Jack Zeigler felt as though he was going around in circles. What he craved was for someone to know that he was doing his best to bring down military and government people. The trouble was that the only person giving him any attention was Tony Signorotto. He needed headlines. He craved notoriety. His drug taking was now beyond excessive and he trusted no-one, and his paranoia now descended on his latest recruit, Mick Gray.

Gray had approached him and offered to do some cleaning around the presbytery which Ziegler accepted gratefully. It was when Gray also offered to do the cleaning of the church that alarm bells started ringing. There was no way Gray could access where the pistol was and he hadn't mentioned anything but the cleaning of the floors and the pews in the church proper. That didn't lower Ziegler's radar though. He willingly handed over the church keys to his new recruit but not before he had removed the small brass key that gave access to the tabernacle. It wouldn't have come as a surprise to Gray because in any church, that particular cabinet was out of bounds to all but the parish priest or one of his appointed religious helpers. In his church he had made sure there were none. Helpers in other areas were fine, but not anywhere up on the altar. Still, there was one thing he could try and do.

When Ziegler was overseas on active duty, one of the things he was allowed to do was contact relatives of any personnel that he gave any help to in relation to their wellbeing whilst on active duty. He would quite often contact relatives of his flock and inform them on how their son or daughter was going. In this way, the Army was being quite open and supportive and hopefully not be criticised in one of the mental health areas that was important to the families. He had been given an access code to get details of members, which on his leaving the forces had been cancelled, but he had also, through an open computer that a fellow pastor had left on a desk, gained access to his compatriot's code. He had written it down but had never used it. This other pastor was still overseas on deployment. He knew that with little effort, he could find out details on Mick Gray. It would be a one-off use because the access would set off red flags once the database realised it had not come from a proper military enquiry based overseas.

He walked slowly from his Carlton church and headed to the Carlton library near Curtain Square. He was not about to make a rookie mistake of logging in through his own account.

He stopped for a take-away coffee at the hole in the wall shop near the library and slowly walked over to a bench in Curtain Square to sip on his purchase at the same time as having a good look around for anyone that may have followed him. After fifteen minutes, he rose and walked across Rathdowne Street and into the library, taking a seat at a computer terminal where he had a view of the street through a small window. Once settled he got to work with the stolen military code. He knew he would have to be quick because once the system realised it was being used from two countries it would shut down immediately.

It only took a few minutes using the Carlton library information to get into the records area. Punching in the stolen code, he hovered over the keyboard and as soon as it was activated, he typed in the name of Mick Gray. Realising straight away that he should have used the full name of Michael Gray, he did it again.

He was mad at himself for the name mistake, so when the database came up with two Michael Gray's , he tried to read as much as he could, but it was almost impossible to absorb any information without writing it down. He thought he had one of about the same age as his new cleaner but suddenly the screen went blank then started to flash with a red cross all the way over the screen. He had failed.

His paranoia was now at an all-time high. Thumping the computer loudly he swore and stormed out of the library, failing to see the hidden figure of Tony Signorotto in the shadows in the park.

As Ziegler walked off, he threw his newspaper violently into a rubbish bin just as a female walked out briskly from the library and called out to him to come back. Ziegler broke into a trot and disappeared. Signorotto walked quickly over the road, pulled out his Police badge and spoke to the woman.

"What's wrong, what did that man do?"

"He obviously didn't get what he wanted from one of the computers, so he hit it and stormed out. He broke the screen."

"Show me the computer please,"

Once taken inside, he was led to the broken computer. The screen was certainly cracked but Signorotto's face fell when he looked at the still red flashing screen which was denying access to a military database.

"Please don't touch this. I'll get someone to come and collect it and do a report on it."

He immediately rang Max Tyler and arranged for it to be photographed in-situ and then removed to the tech section to be analysed.

Chapter 49

Once the tech section had analysed the broken computer the next day and had reported their findings back to Max Tyler, he quietly relayed the information to Tony Signorotto. On tracing the computer information back to the original entry, it became obvious that Ziegler was trying to gain information on any military member by the name of Mick Gray.

"He obviously has doubts about your inside man at the church, Tony. It looks like there are two entries by the name of Michael Gray, but he was only given five seconds to get any information," Tyler said.

"Just as well, Max. I was wondering what he was going to the library for but when I saw where he was trying to get into, I immediately realised he was digging for information on the name Mick Gray. I've got hold of Brian and advised him to get away from Ziegler as quick as possible. Even though he wouldn't have matched up any records to our false Mick Gray, it goes to show the level of paranoia he's at. Can you get Kate to ring me as soon as she can? I want to set up a meet with her, Rick Hawke and Ben Waite. We just have to get Ben to talk."

"Okay. I'll go downstairs and talk to her. She's pretty busy without you here, but she knows what you are trying to do. We all want this guy locked up before anything else happens."

Ten minutes later, Kate went into her office, closed the door and phoned Tony.

"Hey, boss. You still dogging that creep Ziegler?" Kate said with a serious tone in her voice.

"Sure am, Kate and I'm convinced this guy is going to do something else real soon. Yesterday I found out that he was trying to obtain info on the guy that I have planted at his church. What we have to do is get Ben talking. He is the central cog in this. If he'll come out of his shell and talk about the night Billy was killed. We need a direct link to Ziegler. Anything that Billy said to Ben. Anything at all from that last night. How's he been at your place?"

"He's calmed down a lot. Tom has got him working at his security firm, washing the cars and doing general jobs. He's started to talk to a few of the lads there and seems to be settling in," Kate said.

"We need to bring him into Dom's for a sit down. There must be something that will set him off against Ziegler. He can't pretend that it will all just go away. I think the best way to jolt him back into the world is maybe for an accidental sighting between him and Ziegler. What do you think about me getting Rick to contact Ziegler on some pretext of reconciliation and have him meeting him at Dom's place? Ziegler will walk in, and not only would Rick be there but I'll be there with Ben. Ziegler is aware that I am after him. He will probably really act up. We need to convince Ben that Ziegler will not go away unless we get him for the shootings. We have the shell casings from Billy's death, the bullets that were let fly at Galbraith and we have his prints from the back of Simon Forbes's car. If we can get Ben to give us any more links in relation to the night Billy was shot, then we can grab him."

"You'll have to let Rick know that it's a set-up otherwise if he's having coffee with Ben and Ziegler walks in, then there could be fireworks."

"I want fireworks, but from Ziegler. I want him to threaten Rick for setting up a false meeting. All his nightmares might show when he sees us all. We have to stop pussy footing around before he hits another target," Signorotto said with a serious tone.

"All right, let me know where and when. Tom might drive him in for back-up. They get on really well, both being ex-military. I'll word him up on the quiet. I've got to get back onto the job now. How long have you been told to take leave for, Tony?"

"I think till this is all put to rest. Looking on the positive side I hope to be back running the ship very soon."

"Just be really careful, mate. On one hand you're dogging a bloke who I think is mentally unbalanced and you'll have Ben there who is still suffering from a huge dose of PTSD. Then there's the other one who hasn't fully recovered in my mind," Kate said pointedly.

"Who? Rick is pretty good now according to Dom."

"Not Rick. I'm talking about you."

Signorotto said nothing.

Chapter 50

Brian Gold had been given the 'heads up' by Tony Signorotto about Ziegler's attempted name search on 'Mick Gray' at the library so he made up his mind to get out from under what he could see was Ziegler's mounting suspicion about him.

He had been able to have a good look around the church while he cleaned it. Some of the parishioners had relaxed in his company because unlike the pastor, Brian had not been given to shouting down the government or anyone connected to the Veterans. The usual two or three elderly parishioners who took care of things like flowers for the altar, the distribution of church materials in the pews and general odd jobs were slowly forthcoming about Ziegler. The general opinion of him was definitely a person who was prone to sudden bouts of bad temper and yelling, which, in recent times had scared some of them that much that a number of them had departed his church, never to return. The ones that remained were quite elderly and couldn't face the prospect of not only finding another church but also of the transport problems to get themselves to another parish. Some of them had spoken to Ziegler about his constant ranting and raving against authority together with the way he spoke to and treated some of the longer serving members of the parish, but it had all fallen on deaf ears. Two of them had even written to the archbishop and were awaiting a reply. In the meantime, they just got on with looking after their one-hundred-year-old church building. One fact that Brian did note was that no parishioner had ever been asked into the presbytery house for even a cup of tea, which was a tradition with all previous ministers. Ziegler was a one man show. With this ongoing open door policy regarding Veterans being allowed to stay, one of the longest serving parishioners had likened the church to a military compound and went as far as saying it reminded him of Waco Texas albeit before the siege.

A couple of days after Signorotto had warned Brian to be on his toes, he put his set of church keys on the kitchen table and quietly left, but not before leaving Ziegler a note saying that it was time for him to move on. It was a nice note thanking Ziegler for his hospitality and wishing him well with his future endeavours. He had helped Tony as much as he could without putting himself in a no-win situation such as going on some sort of recognizance with Ziegler.

On Zeigler's return later that day, his mind exploded on him. Here he was trying to help veterans, and they were deserting him like rats off a sinking ship. Couldn't they understand he was trying to help them by eliminating those that tried to control them. Not for one minute did he think back to the fact that he was trying to discover if 'Mick Gray' was even a legit veteran and that he, Jack Zeigler, was also one of those who tried to control them.

Through some illicit dealings in the shadows of the city food caravan, he had managed to get hold of a cocktail of drugs. Not only was he now popping Ritalin tablets but was also doing lines of cocaine with some ecstasy. He thought it would help to keep him alert and firing on all cylinders, but it was only feeding his paranoia to the extent that he now thought everyone was his enemy. He sat at the presbytery kitchen table sweating, his mind racing at the same time as he tore Mick Gray's note to shreds and let it fall on the floor. Suddenly there was a loud knock at the door which made him jump up, leaving some of his drug paraphernalia on the table. Thinking that it was Gray making an apologetic return, he snatched open the front door only to be confronted by an elderly man dressed in a suit with a religious collar, gold chain and crucifix around his neck. Ziegler's mind could not focus on the situation.

"Who are you? What do you want?"

The man looked at him for what seemed like minutes but was in actual fact only seconds. With a questioning look on his face he spoke in a concise and clipped tone.,

"You have met me before, Jack. I am your Bishop, Reverend

147

Ian Mulgrew. I've come to talk to you about your parish work. I have emailed you quite a few times, but you haven't responded. It's time we had a chat. Let's step inside, eh," the bishop said noting the unshaved and sweating face of his curate.

Before Ziegler realised, Mulgrew was past him and heading towards the kitchen. Realising he had left his various drugs on the table, he pushed past him and grabbing the tablets and drug gear, he picked them up, went to the rubbish bin and threw them hurriedly into it hoping all the while that Mulgrew hadn't noticed. Mulgrew had. He leant down and retrieved some of the drugs and put them back onto the table.

"Sit down Jack. It's time for a complete review of your spiritual and communal life here at the Church of the Uniting Spirit. I have, as I said, sent you emails inquiring about some serious complaints I have had from various parishioners. First off, why haven't you responded to my emails?"

Jack Ziegler's mind was operating on a different level to the bishop's. He hadn't looked at any of his parish emails for weeks, but he now didn't seem to care. The parish pulpit was his soap box from where he spoke out and that was all that mattered. He ran his fingers through his hair as one foot constantly tapped on the floor. With one free hand he played with the small bottle of Ritalin.

"You have no idea what work I do here, especially for my fellow returned service people. All you are interested in is preaching the so-called word of your God. That's not helping my people at all," Ziegler said in a low threatening tone which made the bishop move his chair back slightly.

"Jack, I have parishioners saying that you do nothing but scream about the government at every chance you get. They are saying that you look drugged a lot of the time and now that I've seen what's on the table I must say I would have to believe them. You look dishevelled and the pupils of your eyes are like pinpoints. I think you need to seek some doctor's advice for what you are taking here. Do you have an old injury or is it some form of PTSD from your service days?" a concerned Mulgrew said.

Ziegler stood and paced the floor trying to calm himself down in front of a person who he considered to be just as conceited and ignorant as the military ones. Turning abruptly, he looked down on the bishop who was still seated.

"This is my church and I will do as I please here. I would suggest that you remove yourself before I lose my temper with you," a screaming Ziegler spat at his Bishop.

Mulgrew wisely stood and walked quickly to the front door before he spoke.

"Pastor Jack Ziegler, you will quit these premises and this parish. If you are not out of here within one week, the police will be called. I am also revoking your Ministry as a member of this Diocese. This church is now out of your hands," Mulgrew said ducking as a statue of an angel smashed into the door jamb just above his head after being hurled by a now completely out of control Jack Ziegler.

Chapter 51

Tony Signorotto was leaning up against a shiny kitchen food preparation bench at Dom Santino's restaurant in Lygon Street. He had his arms folded across his big chest as he talked to Max Tyler in hushed tones.

Dom himself wasn't coming in till later in the afternoon for the busy Friday evening service, but Signorotto had already been in contact with him about using the kitchen for a meeting that would include Rick Hawke. The last thing he wanted to do to Rick was to put too much pressure on him when they brought up the urgent need to get Ben to tell them what they knew, so he thought that a chat in Rick's place of work would make him feel more comfortable. At the end of the day, Hawke was still a veteran with problems and even though he had a steady job and was getting back into everyday life he could still be pretty fragile.

Being a Friday, there would be quite a few workers coming in for their end of week pasta 'hits' together with a glass or two of Chianti over a long lunch so Signorotto had made his apology over the phone to Dom earlier that morning. As per usual, Dom was fine with anything Signorotto did.

"No problems, Tony. Rick went out last night so he's not starting till about ten. I will tell Silvana that you are using your 'special' meeting room and to give Rick a decent amount of time to talk to you. I would like him ready to do table service by about eleven-thirty though."

"What's Silvana doing here today?" Tony said inquiringly. "More to the point, what's Rick doing serving tables. I thought he was kitchen staff?"

"It's only been a short time, I know, but Rick has the restaurant thing in his blood. Turns out he is distantly related to my old friend Frank Arcuri who used to own The Spaghetti Spot up the other end of Lygon Street. Rick is loving not only his work but since I have had Silvana in here learning the business, and on a lot of days doing it single handedly, I think they might have more than a mutual love for linguini going on. I know I talked to you a fair while ago about coming into the business with me, but I knew your heart wasn't really in it. Turns out that Silvana offered. I didn't put her up to it, but she just loves the business side of things. Never know my old *paisano* it might read *Dom and daughter* over the front door soon. It's time I took my beautiful wife on a long trip back to the homeland. None of us, including you, can go on forever. Carlton will be here long after you and I have been laid to rest in the Carlton cemetery."

"Not for me, my friend. I'm going to have my ashes scattered over at Princes Park. I couldn't afford a plot in Melbourne General. "

"Ah, you and I know they don't do that at football grounds anymore," a laughing Dom Santino replied.

"Maybe so, but I still have a lot of contacts in the Police Air Wing. Amazing what goes on in a Police helicopter at three in the morning in between car chases. Anyway, enough talk of death. We won't hold Rick up long. It's just that we need his help in trying to end the spate of military shootings and murders around Carlton," Signorotto said before ending the call after a friendly goodbye.

Just before ten, Signorotto saw Rick Hawke coming down the stairs outside in the small rear courtyard. Close behind was Silvana Santino. A big smile broke out on his face as he thought back on when Silvana and her two sisters played in the courtyard as children.

Oh, how time flies, he thought.

Rick looked up in surprise at the three police members.

"Good morning Rick and a good morning to you too, Silvana," Signorotto said smiling as he watched the girl's face begin to turn bright red. "Must be the hot Italian blood, eh Silvana?"

"You won't say......" she said before Signorotto cut her off.

"What? That you have fallen for this big ex-soldier. Not a word. Now if you don't mind Silvana, we need to have a chat with Rick. Now that you are running the restaurant you probably have stuff to do in the office, eh?"

Silvana rushed up and gave Signorotto a big hug before heading off. He turned and spoke to Hawke.

"You break her heart and all your old SAS tricks in the world won't save you from me, understand?" Signorotto said in a serious tone.

"Tony, that girl has given me a whole new life. What we want to do is gradually take the restaurant over from Dom. He has run this place for probably thirty years and deserves a slower life for himself and his wife Maria. He told the girls that he wants to take a long trip back to Italy, so Silvana has stepped up to be manager and I am going to take over the restaurant floor hopefully. I haven't been here long, but I love this life. The Santino family has been so kind to me. In answer to your veiled threat, I think you can treat me and Silvana as a bit of an item now."

"That's great news, mate. It could work out really well for all of you. In the meantime though we have a bit of a situation we need to fix real quick and the only way the department will do it is if some really hard evidence can be found against Ziegler and, to take it one step further, we need to get Ben Waite talking. You on board for an idea?" Signorotto said.

"Tony, I'll do anything to stop that maniac. I got a bit of a heads up yesterday from Kate when she dropped in for a coffee. How can I help?" Hawke said.

"Well, let's all sit down and we'll go on with the plan," Signorotto said as they headed to the back of the nearly empty restaurant and sat down. Max Tyler took over.

"First off, Rick, Tony here is not allowed anything to do with the situation. Technically it has been taken over by the Homicide Squad, but they are up to their eyeballs in bodies from other jobs and have sort of given me and unofficially, Tony, the nod to keep digging. Tony has been told to take some time off but what the bosses don't know, they don't need to know.

He has come up with an idea to try and goad Ziegler. Basically, we want you to contact him and sort of say that you wouldn't mind sitting down with him as what you're doing now sucks and you blame the government for not letting you get on with your life. Not too over the top, but enough to spur him on to keep up his tirade. We really need info on the gun that was used."

"Yeah, Kate mentioned that. What makes you think that he'll want me back on board though?" Hawke said.

"Well, a person that I dropped in as a plant on him has now left his church because his cover was about to be blown. Ziegler has a big ego and if you sort of make a grovelling come- back then that will really stroke his ego," Signorotto said.

"We all know that Ben knows something about the night Billy McKay was killed. We believe that Ben saw Billy follow Ziegler that night and that Ziegler shot him. Same slugs have been used in all the shootings. Ben is too scared to say anything. We have to turn him around," Max chipped in. "Sounds terrible, but what sort of threat from Ziegler to Ben would upset Ben, do you think?" Max said straight to Rick's face.

"I think just seeing Ziegler would scare Ben. I think Ben will keep his time at the church to himself as long as it looks like Ziegler isn't going to harm him. As far as he is concerned, he wants Ziegler staying in his church and a long way from him. Ben doesn't care about who he tries to recruit, as long as he isn't coming back after him. I've had a couple of coffee catchups with him, and he just wants the status quo to continue. Him in one world and Ziegler in another. I'm sure as police officers you know all about PTSD. After all, as the saying goes, soldiers go to war, police go to war every day. I still wake up with the night sweats about what I did over there, but Ben wakes up with night sweats about Ziegler coming after him more than what happened in his overseas deployment."

"Well, none of us here want to add to his troubles so we are going to have to nut out something," Signorotto said just as his mobile phone rang. Kate McLaren's name flashed up on the screen.

"Hi Kate. What's up? Just having a chat with Rick at the

moment."

"Have a Bishop Mulgrew at the station. You'd better meet with him. It's vital."

"In relation to what?"

"Your nemesis, Jack Ziegler."

"Tell him I'll swing by in ten minutes, and we can talk in my car."

Chapter 52

Tony Signorotto pulled up as quietly as he could outside the police station, even though he was in his old and loud GT Falcon. Getting out, he approached the Bishop who was obvious not only by his nervous demeanour but also because of the white religious 'dog collar' and gold chain with a cross that was swinging from side to side of his jacket as he paced back and forth.

Tony Signorotto introduced himself to the Bishop. "I'm the Senior Sergeant in Charge of Carlton. Just taking a few weeks off at the moment. Kate McLaren probably told you I have an interest in Jack Ziegler."

"Yes, she did," a very concerned looking Mulgrew said. "I have actually come here because I have some serious concerns in relation to him and his service at one of my parishes."

"What's he done that makes you so concerned? Before you answer that though, I must tell you that I and some other senior members have been keeping a very close eye on him in relation to some serious crimes that have happened around Carlton."

"Well, I have just been at his presbytery about emails I have received from quite a few parishioners and I must say not replied to by him about his sermons and behaviour. Also in relation to ex-service people staying at the church."

"Bishop, I would like you to come into the station if you would. Let's have a coffee and I'll tell you the whole story of why the Department is interested in him. You okay with that?"

"Looks like I'm about to find out information that could seriously affect The Church of the Holy Spirit."

"It could and probably will affect your church as a whole," Signorotto said leading him to the front door of the station.

Signorotto left him seated in the foyer as he instructed one of the counter staff to get Kate McLaren to come down which she did almost immediately."

"Kate, we know they have put me on leave but it is imperative that I speak to this person in an interview room. I think the whole Jack Ziegler situation is about to explode. If anyone asks, I'm just in here talking to the local Bishop who has dropped in as an old friend, alright."

"No problem at all, Tony. This business of you being sent on leave has to stop. You, Max and James Collins are the only ones across this. We have to end this bullshit about you not being allowed anywhere near Ziegler," Kate said in a furious tone as she indicated to Tony to take the Bishop into the front interview room. "Go and have a chat to your friend."

Signorotto quickly led Mulgrew into the room and closed the door. Kate in the meantime strode into her office and dialled the number for the Homicide Squad.

"Homicide Squad front desk. How can I help?" a young female voice said.

"Senior Sergeant Kate McLaren from Carlton here. I want to speak to one of your crew members who is supposedly looking into the murders of Simon Forbes and Billy McKay. I need to speak to one ASAP."

"Stand by. I think that is crew three. You'll be speaking to Detective Senior Sergeant Bryce Jones." A minute went by before the call was picked up.

"Bryce Jones, Kate. What's up?"

"Look, I know you've given a bit of a loose rein to Tony Signorotto in relation to this Carlton situation, but we've just had the local Bishop in here and he's talking to Tony in the interview room about something that has happened with Ziegler. I don't want Tony getting in deeper that he has with this without him being put back fully operational and thus being officially involved. I might be stepping on toes here but Tony knows more about this than you guys and knows Carlton more than anyone I know. Can you do something about getting him back on board and can you get down here and get up to speed. If Tony goes right after Ziegler and gets into the shit it will end him for sure."

"Kate, my boss went up yesterday to the AC Crime's office because the guy who put Tony on leave has gone on long service leave himself and the braid that has taken over has been fully briefed with a view to getting Tony back in the fold. I'll come over straight away so if you can have a quick chat to Tony and let him know I'm coming and he can arrange for this Bishop to stay put. Tony has been letting us know what he's been up to and it's time everything was made above board. I'll get over there within thirty minutes. This might be something we can use as leverage with Ziegler. Hold tight. I'll try and get an update on Tony's position as well. Hopefully some good news."

Kate went down quickly, knocked on the interview room, got Tony out into the foyer and explained what she had done. Tony looked at her directly and then smiled widely.

"Thanks, Kate. I just feel we are getting somewhere now. The Bishop has just told me about Ziegler exploding at being told he has been suspended from church duties and has a week to get out of the parish. Ziegler's a time bomb. I've just started to tell him about some of my beliefs about his Pastor but I might wait and see how he reacts when the Homicide boys give him some facts. Just get someone to get some coffee in here, will you. It might be a long session."

Kate walked away hoping she had done the right thing but she quickly decided she had. Although Tony was still recovering mentally from being shot months before, she knew that the only way was to let him get fully involved.

Nothing would stop that pig headed Italian, anyway.

Chapter 53

By the time Bryce Jones walked into the interview room and introduced himself to Mulgrew, he could see that the Bishop was certainly taken aback by any information that Signorotto had given Mulgrew. The man sat there with an ashen face.

"Just need to speak to Tony for a minute, Bishop. We'll be right back," Jones said quietly as he indicated to Signorotto to join him outside the room.

"Tony, first things first. The temporary AC Crime has given you permission to come back off leave and run the station again, which means that you can be involved officially with this investigation. He's also got Superintendent Collins back on board as Divisional Superintendent. The Deputy Commissioner's office ran a little investigation and found out that our friend who is on leave is a big donor to the church diocese and couldn't stand the thought that a Minister may be involved. He had heard a few whispers coming down about your methods and didn't want any blowback. It looks like he has taken all his long service leave with a view to retirement at the end of it, which will probably be a few months away. Anyway, I got the phone call on the way over here, so you are back on board with the proviso that you do nothing without running it past me. I'm more than happy to have you do all the legwork you want, but if it comes to grabbing Ziegler or there being a big confrontation, then my crew will step in. That suit you?" Jones said.

"Absolutely. I have told Mulgrew a fair bit of what we suspect, but only enough to keep Ziegler at arm's length. What he came to tell me was that he visited Ziegler this morning to talk about complaints from the parishioners. When he got inside, he saw a lot of drugs that Ziegler was trying to hide. When he questioned him about the parishioners' complaints, which Ziegler never even bothered to answer, he got extremely agitated and demanded Mulgrew leave, even throwing a statue at him.

Mulgrew decided there and then to suspend him from all parish duties and has asked him to leave the church within a week. He's actually putting him out on the street, would you believe," Signorotto said.

"How close are we to nabbing him, do you think, Tony?" Jones said earnestly.

"We have to turn Ben Waite into a witness. Rick Hawke, the other resident at the church, is going to try and get Ziegler to meet up. He is going to tell him he is sick of working for peanuts as a dishwasher at a restaurant and wants a much better deal from the government because of his PTSD. Unfortunately, we are going to have to throw Ben to the wolves a bit to scare him into telling us what we need. I was about to run this past Rick before I got the call from Kate. I came down here straight away."

"What sort of meeting?"

"Just one at a local park. Max and I are going to be having a coffee with Ben, and we will get Rick to be on a bench nearby for his meeting. When they get together, I am going to 'accidentally' walk Ben past them. Rick will act surprised, and I think Ziegler will go off at Ben when he sees him. I'll whisk Ben away and act surprised."

"A lot of maybes and hoping in the plan, Tony," Jones said, scratching at the back of his neck.

"Rick Hawke believes that Ben won't say a word about the night Billy McKay was murdered as long as Ziegler stays out of his world. By doing this, we will be able to tell him that the only way this could happen is for Ziegler to be put away for life."

"When are you going to do it?"

"As soon as Rick can make a date with Ziegler. With Ziegler having to get out of the church very soon, he will feel abandoned, but with Rick coming back to him, you never know."

"How about we explain the whole scenario to Mulgrew and get him to give Ziegler two weeks' grace? We can have the undercovers just stay all over him like a blanket. Maybe getting Rick to tell Ziegler that the whole DVA set-up needs shaking up again," Jones said.

Signorotto thought for a moment before speaking.

"I know this is out of left-field thinking, but what if we somehow got Peter Galbraith to say something about his attempted murder and that if the shooter was good enough, he would not have missed in the first place."

"You mean Galbraith saying this in the newspaper?" a surprised-looking Jones said.

"Not in the newspapers, but how about getting him onto A Current Affair this week and follow it up in the newspapers? Ziegler told my man that he had unfinished business with Galbraith. Being in the Homicide squad, surely you have some people in the media who are always chasing a story?" Signorotto said.

"Yeah, got a few I'd trust. I'd have to see if it's okay with Galbraith, though. He'd have to be minded around the clock if Ziegler went for it," Jones said.

"If Rick can arrange the meeting, he can drop in that 'the guy from DVA is going on the TV," Signorotto said. "First things first, we need Ben to give us some evidence, then we do the Galbraith thing."

"I'll go and see Galbraith; you get that meeting happening."

"Let's talk to Mulgrew," Jones said as they opened the interview room door.

Chapter 54

Two days later, Bryce Jones rang Tony Signorotto, who was now back in control at Carlton and back in his favourite uniform of blue.

"I've had to pull in a few future favours, but I've managed to get us a small gig on A Current Affair this coming Wednesday, and I have been in contact with Peter Galbraith, who is willing to do anything to get this guy. As far as he's concerned, anything to protect his people in the armed services is okay. He knows the risk of his house being attacked again, so right after the interview, he is putting himself up at the Melbourne Club for a week. Even if Ziegler went after him, there is no way he will get past the front door."

"That's good. Now that Mulgrew's agreed to extend Ziegler's time at the church, it might work out. Rick rang Ziegler, and they agreed to meet in Curtain Square at the Canning Street end at ten thirty tomorrow morning. It's not a coffee or anything. Rick told him it had to be quick, because he had to go back to work in that 'shitty' coffee shop in Lygon Street," Signorotto said, referring to Dom's restaurant.

"What about your meeting with Ben Waite?"

"Set for ten up at the Rathdowne end of the Square. Grabbing a coffee at the Kent Hotel. We'll be off the street, but I'll be able to see where Rick sits. There's a bench about three quarters of the way down the park. He's going to pocket prank me when he wants us to walk down."

"Do you want anyone else around to back you up, just in case things get nasty?" Jones said.

"No. I'll have Max Tyler floating around, but I can't see Ziegler being anything more than his arrogant self if he's trying to get Rick back in his clutches. Once he sees Ben with me, it'll take a few seconds to realise that, for some reason, he is in the middle of some sort of set-up. I want to time it so Rick has finished and has walked away before I parade Ben past him. He definitely won't like seeing me, so he'll be a bit confused once he's seen his past lodgers and me all within the space of a few minutes.

"Rick is going to have to drop the Current Affair bit on him virtually straight after he says he wants back in," Jones said.

"Rick has it planned that he's going to go off about Galbraith being an arrogant prick because he's seen the ad about him going on TV and that he's had enough of blokes like him grabbing the headlines instead of working for the veterans. Galbraith is going to come across as untouchable. I'd like to be a fly on the presbytery wall when Ziegler watches the show. You don't know how many 'heads up' stories I will owe this contact of mine, so I hope and pray it all comes around."

Chapter 55

Although it was a plan that had been gone over many times in their heads, Rick Hawke still had sweaty palms as he sat on the bench in Curtain Square. He had checked his phone on numerous occasions to make sure he had Signorotto's phone number ready for a 'pocket' dial.

He believed the call he had made to Ziegler had been reasonably harmonious, but he felt the pastor's voice go up a notch or two with interest when he got to the crux of why he had rung. He had been briefed by Signorotto that he would have Max Tyler nearby in case things got out of hand.

At the arranged time, Hawke saw Ziegler approaching along the path at a reasonable pace. Hawke did not stand or offer a handshake to him. What he did, though, was switch on the micro cassette recorder he had concealed in his shirt. He did notice, however, that Ziegler looked very nervous as he stood in front of him, constantly twitching his face as though he was trying to get rid of flies or similar.

"You called me, Rick. What's this about?" Ziegler said in a voice that was stopping short of sounding authoritative. Hawke wasn't going to muck around. He had been given the ideal opening.

"I saw an ad for a show on TV that really annoyed me. In fact, it pissed me off completely and made me think about what you were going on about back when I stayed at the church with Billy McKay and Ben Waite."

Ziegler suddenly sat down on the bench next to Hawke.

"What are you talking about? What show?" an intrigued Ziegler replied.

"That Peter Galbraith is going to be on A Current Affair on Thursday night. He's being interviewed about his position in charge of Veteran Affairs."

"So? The arrogant prick will probably try and justify what he does. Just another fat pig with his snout in a government trough.

No real surprise. He's lucky he's still around to give an interview," Ziegler said with a wry smile on his face.

"The ad clip showed him talking about the attempted hit on him a while back," Hawke said, watching Ziegler's face closely.

Ziegler seemed to stiffen in his posture.

"What did he say? That he was shit scared?" Ziegler said sarcastically.

"Far from it. He was basically calling out the, as he said, 'pathetic individual' that didn't have the guts to face him man to man. That he popped a few shots into his house and ran away like the coward he was. It was like an invitation to have another go. Such an arrogant bastard. He needs a good belting. Sprouting off about what a load of work he does for Vet Affairs. I'm starting to agree with you, Jack, that he needs bringing down a peg or two. Why should I work in some little restaurant for peanuts while blokes like him get paid a fortune and do very little for us," Hawke said, all the while looking at Ziegler, whose face was turning bright red as well as showing a snarl.

"He actually fucking said I was a coward?" Ziegler exploded as he jumped up off the bench.

"What do you mean, you?" Hawke said with a flash of surprise as Ziegler realised he had gone too far.

"Didn't mean me. What I meant to say was, did he call whoever the shooter was a coward?"

"Yeah. Pretty pathetic from behind a TV lens," Hawke said as he pressed his pocketed phone to give Tony Signorotto a heads-up that he had dropped the TV bit on Ziegler. "It just shows the arrogance of that Vet Affairs department," Hawke said with a furious tone in his voice.

Ziegler began pacing back and forth before breaking into a tirade about anything and everything in relation to the Federal Government and Veteran Affairs in particular.

"None of these assholes have ever done what you and I did, Rick. They never served their country and underwent the nightmares of war. Not like us. Not like real soldiers. They should all be shot. They all should be gotten rid of," he screamed at no one in particular.

It was then that Rick Hawke figured out Jack Ziegler and why he had such a hatred for those in government and, in particular, those in charge of the armed services. It was because he thought he was an actual soldier who had seen battle, even though he had just been a Minister back at base camp. He had spoken to so many service personnel coming through his ministry that he had somehow convinced himself that he was a real soldier too. In his own mind, he had put himself in their shoes. He had blended into this quasi-style soldier. Hawke had a dislike for the 'barracks heroes' as much as many serving troops did, but this was different. Whereas there would always be people who 'talked the talk' but never 'walked the walk,' this had escalated way above that. Ziegler had convinced himself that it was his job to atone for the sins of the Army. Ziegler was now a dangerous psych case that was on his one-man mission to avenge. To write the wrongs. To fix things. Ziegler was basically a dangerous, delusional psychopath.

As Hawke watched Ziegler morph into some sort of avenging warrior, out of the corner of his eye, he saw Tony Signorotto approach with Ben Waite.

"What are you?...." Ben said to Rick before looking up and seeing and hearing Ziegler ranting about getting even with the world. Ben froze on the spot as he grabbed hold of Signorotto's arm.

"Shit, Ben. I didn't know he would be here," indicating Ziegler, who by this stage had turned in their direction and was looking directly at Ben. "Let's just get out of here."

Rick Hawke stood and spoke directly at Ziegler.

"You're completely mad. You call me here for some stupid reason, and you just rant and rave about people. I'm getting out of here right now. I've got no idea what you are on about," he said, turning and walking past Signorotto and Waite whilst giving Tony a surreptitious nod as if to say that he had set Ziegler off completely. The only thing Ben Waite was now concentrating on was the fact that Jack Ziegler was not out of his life at all.

Ziegler looked at Rick Hawke with a look of bewilderment on

his face before speaking.

"You fucking called me, Hawke. What the fuck are you going on about? As for you, you snivelling little coward, Waite, you're a disgrace to the uniform you once wore. What are you doing here with him?" indicating Signorotto. "What's going on here? This some sort of set-up? You're not allowed anywhere near me, Signorotto. This will be reported."

Signorotto kept hold of Waite by the arm as he led the confused and very scared veteran away. Hawke was already on the other side of the park, standing with Max Tyler. He wanted to say something to Ziegler, who was still standing, staring at them, but he knew better. The last thing he wanted was Ziegler running after them.

Max Tyler indicated to them to keep walking past him.

"It's okay. He's not coming. Just standing there wondering how all his enemies have turned up at once."

Signorotto handed the shaking Ben Waite over to Rick Hawke and immediately dialled Bryce Jones, who picked up straight away.

"Had a drone up and saw the whole thing from the black van over to your right."

Signorotto spun around and saw Jones calling him over to the open side door of a Toyota van parked nearby. Another member was next to him, packing up a large drone and putting it back into its case. Signorotto and the others walked over to him.

"Sneaky bastard, Jones. You didn't tell me about putting up a drone?"

"A drone with a microphone and recorder. Got every word, even him pretending that he didn't shoot at Peter Galbraith."

"While Rick Hawke talked quietly to Waite, Signorotto asked Jones a question.

"What next, Bryce?"

"Round-the-clock surveillance on Peter Galbraith's house. I think Ziegler has tripped completely."

Rick Hawke came across to the two of them.

"Think Ben wants to have a word with you lot," he said with a smile on his face.

Chapter 56

Ben Waite sat in the back seat of Bryce Jones's unmarked police car next to Tony Signorotto, whilst Jones looked on from the front seat. Waite still looked a bit like a frightened rabbit after seeing Ziegler, but he was more composed than he had been some twenty minutes before. Signorotto spoke first.

"I'm going to be straight with you, Ben. I think we have been pretty good with looking after you since you got out from Ziegler's church, but we really need you to tell us what you know. The fact that you don't want him in your life is one thing, but now we have had two murders which we believe Ziegler committed, let alone other shootings and one attempted murder. The fact of the matter is, Ben, you must give us what you know so we can stop him. That's the bottom line. You have to give us what you know; otherwise, you'll be looking over your shoulder all the time."

Jones and Signorotto sat in silence, looking straight at the lowered head of Waite. It seemed like an eternity before he eventually spoke.

"Why do I have to be the connection for you?" Waite said in desperation.

"We need you to tell us in your own words what happened on the night Billy McKay was murdered. This guy Ziegler has to be stopped. We have evidence, but we need more," Jones said, deliberately leaving out any mention of the pistol they so desperately needed to know about. A court of law could argue that they had led Ben on by mentioning anything about a pistol. They didn't want to be accused of feeding their witness with any information.

"My brain is telling me one thing and my nerves are telling me another, but if I don't get him out of my life, I'll never move forward, so yeah, okay. The night Billy was killed, he had told me that he had already searched through Ziegler's study and had found an old Bible or something that had a pistol sitting in it. The insides had been cut out to fit it. He left it there, but later he told me he had seen Ziegler put the same pistol into the waistband of his jeans and leave early in the morning. Billy wanted me to go with him and follow Ziegler. Mate, I was no use on one leg, and I was too scared to go anyway. Billy followed him after a few minutes. I never saw him again," a now relieved Ben Waite said.

"How did Billy know it was the same pistol?" Jones said.

"We both knew our firearms. He told me it was a Smith and Wesson Ziegler had slid into his jeans, and it was the same one he saw in the cut-out Bible. Billy knew his guns, mate. He was a small arms expert overseas."

"So let's clarify this on record," Jones said, holding out his phone so as to record everything. "You're being recorded now, Billy, and there's myself and Tony Signorotto listening, okay?"

"Okay. On the night Billy McKay was murdered, he had already told me he had seen a Smith and Wesson pistol sitting inside a cut-out Bible or some book inside Ziegler's study. Billy saw him tuck the pistol into his pants the next morning, real early, about two or three, and walk out the door with a hoodie on. Billy told me straight away that he saw Ziegler walk out with the same gun that he had seen in the book. He wanted me to go with him and follow Ziegler, but I refused. Billy never came back."

Jones and Signorotto looked at each other. A tired smile crossed over Signorotto's face.

"All right, Ben. We'll get you back to your digs at Kate McLaren's house, and we'll get a formal statement off you in a couple of days. Ziegler hasn't a clue where you live, but we now have a real link for the shootings. All the rounds in all the shootings were from a nine-millimetre pistol. The night Billy was shot, there were also a lot of rounds fired at a military building nearby. Those slugs matched the one we retrieved from poor Billy," Jones said to the bowed head of Ben Waite.

After he had gotten Max Tyler to drive Ben back home, Tony turned to Jones.

"I think we need an arrest warrant taken out right now for Ziegler and another for a brick-by-brick search of the church. I don't care what anyone in the department says; that church is going to be torn apart. He has used that Smith and Wesson every time, and I don't think he will have gotten rid of it. Let's get back to Carlton and make the arrangements. You agree?"

"Let's get to work."

Thirty minutes later, when both men were back at Carlton and in the middle of making urgent phone calls to Command and others, Kate McLaren walked into the office quickly.

"Are you getting an arrest warrant for Ziegler?" she said to Jones, who was busy on the phone arranging just that. He just nodded back to her as she held up her hand for him to halt his phone call.

Jones held a hand over his mobile phone. "What, Kate?"

"The undercover team got there and found an ambulance crew treating one of the old parishioners. Slight concussion and a black eye."

Jones dropped his arms to his lap as Tony Signorotto stared back in disbelief.

"What happened to him?" Signorotto said quickly.

"Apparently, he saw Ziegler go into the church with some clothes and a bag. He followed him in and watched him go up to the altar, unlock the tabernacle, and bring out what he said looked like a big handgun. Ziegler suddenly turned around and saw him, but before he could get out of his way, he got cracked over the head by him with the gun, and then, as he hit the floor, he got kicked in the face. Ziegler ran out of the church, and the old man he hit saw him get into a taxi and drive off."

"Tell the UCs we'll get there as quick as we can," Signorotto said as he and Jones raced for the door.

Jumping into Jones's car, Signorotto spoke. "He's done a runner for sure."

Chapter 57

The homicide detective and the Senior Sergeant stood looking over the shoulder of the forensic officer as he dusted the tabernacle for prints. One thing they could see was a box of nine-millimetre Winchester brand bullets.

"I'd say that he's pretty incensed about what Rick said to him at the park about Galbraith going on TV. Grabbing a handful of clothes and the pistol smacks of desperation. I think we've lit a fuse with him. He could have stayed here and come up with a plan, but now we have to cover Galbraith around the clock. It's him he's got the set against and I don't reckon he will care what happens to himself. Those drugs on the kitchen table are all over the place," Signorotto said quietly so as not to be overheard by anyone in the forensic team that was going over the altar with a fine-tooth comb. Before they'd come into the church, both members had gone into the presbytery and seen the different types of pill bottles and drug packaging that were strewn across the kitchen table.

"Did you notice the cocaine residue on the glass plate? He's taking anything and everything. That's when the paranoia sets in," Jones said just as the forensic member at the tabernacle turned to them.

"Gents, I can tell you that the only prints anywhere on the inside of this little cabinet are those of Jack Ziegler. They are on the box of ammo too. This has purely been his little domain."

"He didn't even trust the complete set of church keys to your plant Brian Gold, alias Mick Gray," Jones said.

"Now we know why. I should have realised that the only place you wouldn't have dreamed of hiding a firearm was the tabernacle. Never crossed my mind, even when I got Gold to have a good look around here when he was cleaning for Ziegler. I could kick myself."

"Mate, to get a search warrant authorised for this place was hard enough, but the bosses would have stopped short of the altar. Don't beat yourself up over it," Jones said, putting his hand on Signorotto's shoulder.

"What next? We have two days until Galbraith appears on TV. We can't pull him off the interview because Ziegler will suspect something and may even think he has us on the back foot," Signorotto said slowly as he rubbed the back of his neck. "Ziegler has already had one crack at Galbraith at his house. We can put a couple of uniforms in there and let them camp for a few days. Max can get some undercover members for that. Even though he is still staying at the Melbourne Club, we will have to put some members there as well. Our main concern is to cover Galbraith once he comes near the Channel Twelve studio down in Richmond. All-day roadblocks and patrols until the trap is done. We have to remember that even though he served overseas as a chaplain, he did go out on a few sorties with the troops to experience what they felt like in battle, so he'll know a bit about getting close to your enemy with camouflage and the like."

"All hands-on deck at Carlton tomorrow. You, me, Max. I might get Superintendent Collins to come in. I'll let the DC Crime know what's going on, and I'll have to let my TV contact know. Let's hope with the upping of security and police they'll still go ahead," Jones said.

"Tom Cole, Kate's partner, has the security contract for Channel Twelve, so he can join us also. He's ex-SAS, so his brain will be worth picking," Signorotto said. "I'll get onto Division and get the SOG to be in this. They can do the close perimeter stuff."

"Sounds like a plan," Jones said.

One thing they hadn't calculated was the fact that Ziegler wasn't happy with just his Smith and Wesson for a planned retribution. Little did they know that as they spoke, he was in a taxi approaching the Melbourne Pistol Club with the intention of removing his Glock ten-millimetre pistol from the safe. Going out in a blaze of glory appealed to his completely drug-riddled brain.

Chapter 58

Jack Ziegler knew that there was one place that the police would not find him, and that was with the rough sleepers in the city.

Having worked the streets with the down-and-outers for some time now, he had come into contact with quite a few police. They didn't mind coming around to the food vans and saying hello and to wave the flag, so to speak, but what none of them did was actually go and disturb or even talk to any of the homeless on the streets unless there had been a report of trouble.

Ziegler only wanted to spend one night there because he had a military-style plan already laid out. Going to his overnight 'motel', he had made a detour past Peter Galbraith's house in Carlton and saw a number of individuals who were obviously police officers coming and going. His mind, although very addled by his constant drug taking, was telling him that there could be a set-up involved in this. Why would there be police at Galbraith's unless they thought he was being targeted? Had that been a trap back at Curtain Square where Rick Hawke had talked about the TV show? Did they want him going after Galbraith? Well, they were going to get their wish, only he didn't believe that anybody that was after him knew that he was a survivalist. There had been many an occasion back overseas where he had bivouacked with the troops. A lot of them thought they couldn't relate to a pastor who was constantly behind the lines and never saw action. The only way to prove that he knew what they went through was to walk in their shoes. If the police thought he couldn't get near Galbraith at the TV studio, then they were sadly mistaken.

The clothes he had taken from the presbytery were very old and dirty ones he had used to do the church gardening. He had also taken a wig and fake beard from the church store, where they were used once a year for one of the young parishioners to dress up to play one of the Three Wise Men in the Christmas procession. These were now priceless to him as he lay down on some cardboard in an alleyway off Elizabeth Street. With an old army coat covering him up to his chin, all someone could see if they came close enough was what looked like an old, bearded rough sleeper who was trying to sleep. Underneath a bunch of rags that he was using as a pillow were the Glock and the Browning, both with fifteen rounds in each mag. He knew he had left the box of ammunition in the tabernacle, but he didn't care. If he couldn't get Galbraith with the first two shots, then even the other twenty-eight were a waste of time. Then he thought, why not twenty-seven. After all, he needed one for himself.

It was late in the morning when Ziegler thought he heard the scratching of a sewer rat under his coat. He didn't take too much notice of rats because he had slept with far worse in the desert. On more than one occasion he had awoken to the slippery feel of a desert horned viper sliding across his body, which was a far more dangerous animal than a rat.

As he lay half-awake, he suddenly realised that it must have been an awfully strong rat because it was actually lifting his hip off the ground. He quickly rolled over to see a young male in a hoodie sliding out the Glock from under his body. Ziegler immediately grabbed the young thief by his non-weapon forearm.

"I wouldn't do that if I was you," he said with a steely voice to the would-be thief, who had by this time moved the gun to within close proximity of Ziegler's head.

"Hey man. You gonna fuckin' die here," the hooded punk said as he pulled the trigger on the Glock.

Ziegler smiled, letting go of the thief as he whipped out the Browning from underneath his body. "You've got no idea, have you, son? You wouldn't have lasted two minutes in the desert. You are just another useless piece of garbage on this earth that needs eliminating."

The youth looked down at the Glock, realising immediately that there was no bullet in the firing chamber. He quickly tried to slide the mechanism into a firing position, but the pistol was snatched out of his hand and then used to smack him across the nose. He lay on the ground holding both hands to his face as blood seeped through his fingers. Ziegler grabbed the would-be robber by the back of his neck, stood up and dragged him further into the alley.

"Big man, eh? My boys will be here in a minute and then we'll kick your arse and stomp on your fuckin' head. Us CPB's rule here, you old prick," the muffled voice came out from between bloodied hands.

"What might CPB stand for, you raggedy little prick?" Ziegler replied as he looked back down the alley. "I don't see any CPB's coming, do you?"

"City Pack Boys, you fucker. You won't walk away from here," the hooded youth said with as much bravado as he could muster.

"Oh, I know for sure that you won't, you sad piece of shit," Ziegler said as he cocked both the Browning and the Glock and pressed the barrels of each against the knees of the seated and now shaking lad.

"You haven't got the balls…" was all the lad said as the loud noise from both pistols sounded, blowing large holes through the two knees of the now screaming youth.

"You are never going to attack or steal from anyone again, arsehole. In fact, I don't think you will ever walk again without help," Ziegler said as he viciously slammed the youth's head against the brick wall behind him, knocking him almost unconscious.

Ziegler dragged the prone, bleeding youth along the alley to a large dumpster. Picking him up, he threw him into the bin, closed the lid and then removed a chain from around his neck that held a large black and silver crucifix. He slid the crucifix through the lock along with the chain, thus stopping anyone opening it from the inside. A low crying sound emitted from the dumpster.

"Someone may find you before you bleed out, but then again they might not. You couldn't hold a candle to any of my boys from the desert," Ziegler said before adding, "Reverend Jack will pray for your soul."

I'll probably see you in hell, son, he thought before returning to his cardboard motel and sleep.

Chapter 59

Max Tyler phoned Tony Signorotto as soon as he heard what had transpired in the city. The only reason he did was because one of the Melbourne City detectives that worked alongside Tyler had a very good memory.

"I think we have all bases covered for Galbraith's arrival and time at Channel Twelve. Is that what you wanted to talk to me about, Max?" Signorotto replied into the hands-free mobile phone that was attached to the dashboard of his police car.

"No, it's not, Tony. One of the boys from Melbourne City uniform attended a shooting in the city down the Elizabeth Street end early this morning. A young punk that is well known to us was found inside a dumpster with both knees blown away."

"Yeah, well that's the remit for your fellow suits on the morning shift. No offence, Max, but we are up to our eyeballs with trying to get Ziegler. What's this got to do with anything?" a slightly annoyed Signorotto replied quickly.

"One of my offsiders remembered being briefed about Ziegler and his title of Reverend. The only reason this kid was found in the dumpster was because the driver of the garbage truck saw the crucifix from his cab. That dumpster only gets picked up once a month and wasn't due for a pick-up for weeks."

"What crucifix?" Signorotto said as he pulled to a halt on the side of the road, his mind racing with very dark thoughts.

"There was a crucifix holding it closed so no one could open it from the inside. The driver pulled out the cross and chain and heard a whimpering sound from within the bin. When he threw the cover back, he found our boy in a big pool of blood and his knees shot to pieces. Beside the crucifix, it's what the boy said when the morning shift boys pulled him free," Tyler said.

"Go on. What did he say?" Signorotto said with a confused voice.

"Beside swearing like a madman about the guy that did this to him, he said, 'Tell them *Reverend Jack* did it.'" He won't say how he got himself tangled up with Ziegler, but I'd say the kid had tried to roll him and didn't know what he was going up against. He won't walk for a long time, and when he does, I think it will be very slowly. If it wasn't for the truck driver spying the crucifix, I'd say we would have had another murder on our hands," Tyler said to a now stunned Signorotto.

"The other interesting and frightening point that I verified a few minutes ago is that the kid said he was shot with two pistols at once. I've already been onto Ziegler's pistol club, and they told me he was there yesterday and removed his Glock for 'cleaning purposes.'

Tony Signorotto thanked Max for the call and sat in his car, feeling overwhelmed and very, very tired all of a sudden. *Christ, will we ever stop this lunatic!*

Chapter 60

When it came down to it, Jack Ziegler knew he could be walking into a trap. He had a fairly good idea that he was being lured like a fly into a spider's web. There were three places he could possibly find Peter Galbraith, and he had already dismissed the first two.

The first was at his address in Carlton, and he had already seen the amount of police that were there. Even if Galbraith was there, it would be impossible to get into the small terrace house and past who he believed would be specialist protection members, probably from both the Australian Federal Police and the Victoria Police. That was option number one, given a big cross.

The second was either before, during, or after the Channel Twelve appearance. Again, too many people and too big a building. He might make it inside, but he had no doubt he would be challenged before he could get near his target.

The third was where he thought he had a chance. By sheer luck, he had seen Galbraith go in and out of the Melbourne Club on several occasions when he had followed him before he had tried to kill him the first time outside of his house. In fact, on three occasions of trailing him, he had seen Galbraith enter the Melbourne Club, and only once had he seen him exit again on the same night. On the other two days, he had observed the Veteran Affairs head go in with a small overnight bag. He had come out again after nine o'clock the next morning on both of those occasions.

After a night of sleeping rough near Elizabeth Street, he made his way up to Collins Street and settled in opposite the Melbourne Club and just waited. Hours went by, but his patience paid off. It was the Thursday night of his appearance on Channel Twelve, and Ziegler had hit pay dirt. Just before lunch, a plain police car had pulled up outside the prestigious club at thirty-six

Collins Street. Galbraith got out holding the same small R.M. Williams duffel bag that he had previously used on overnight stays. He thanked the two plain-clothes police officers and made his way inside. One of the two police raised a portable radio to his mouth, and after a minute or two, a third police member made his way around from Exhibition Street. After a quick chat, the member went back the way he had come.

Ziegler walked slowly across Collins Street and then, without letting the police officer see him, he followed him down Exhibition Street and then around into Little Collins Street. Giving him some distance, he saw the police officer turn right and enter Club Lane. This was the back entrance to the Melbourne Club.

Ziegler walked along to the corner of Westwood Place, to where there was a multistorey car park. Taking the lift to the third level, he exited and walked over to where the car park looked directly into the garden area of the Melbourne Club.

Looking down into the garden was like looking into a nineteenth-century wonderland of tall palm trees, small ponds, and old-style park benches. The narrow pathways in the yard were paved with old red bricks, and the edgings were continuous curved lines of small, angled terracotta tiles. The high red brick wall that was the boundary to Little Collins Street was topped with broken glass set in concrete. Another way of separating the gentry from the plebs. Ziegler could just imagine the members of this elitist club strolling around the paths, whisky in one hand and cigar in the other, discussing wool prices in the Western District of Victoria. It infuriated him even more when he thought about some of the army generals and such who were members of this so-called elitist class. They were the ones who should be grovelling in the sands of Iraq.

After looking down into the yard for ten minutes or so, Ziegler went back down to ground level and searched out a 7-Eleven store where he purchased two bottles of water, some packets of chips, and two burnt-looking sausage rolls. With all this bagged up, he headed back up into the car park and ate the food. It was now just after two o'clock in the afternoon, so he decided to hide in a corner and try to sleep for a couple of hours after checking first that he had some Ritalin tablets to take later on for the job in hand after dark. He made himself comfortable on an old cardboard packing.

The last time you are heard from will be tonight, Galbraith. Don't count on any sweet dreams when you return, though.

***

His body clock was never going to allow him to have more than a light sleep, what with the high levels of different drugs he still had in his system from his stash back at the presbytery. When he woke, he checked his watch and saw that it was just past four o'clock. He knew that Galbraith was going to air at seven-thirty, so he wanted to see him leave the Melbourne Club. Then, after about two hours, just as darkness fell, he would put his plan into action.

Walking back via Little Collins Street and so as not to arouse any suspicion, he went up to Spring Street and then along to Collins Street, where he crossed the road and settled into a doorway to await Galbraith's departure. It was about five-thirty when he noticed the two police members get out of the same car that had brought Galbraith to the Melbourne Club and position themselves on the footpath. Within minutes, his prey had walked down the steps and got into the back seat of the unmarked police vehicle. Ziegler slid back into the shadows as the two police officers had one final look around as they waited for their third member to come around from Exhibition Street before getting into their car and departing, heading in the direction of Channel Twelve.

Ziegler returned to the car park, which was now closed for the night. The cars in there belonged to businesses around the area and were used for transport during the day. There was one floor which you could only gain access to twenty-four hours a day, and that was part of the ground floor. This was used exclusively for members of the Melbourne Club, who all had their own private access cards to let themselves in and out. Approximately fifty metres away on the ground floor was the office for the day shift car park operator. It was a small space with a window on one side. The advantage for Ziegler was that it also contained a small TV set. He quietly broke the lock on the door and settled inside on the floor, placing the TV set beside him. He turned it on to Channel Twelve and waited for Galbraith's interview.

Chapter 61

Between the Special Operations Group, members of the Homicide Squad, and a few hand-picked uniform members with Tony Signorotto, the Channel Twelve TV studios in Richmond were blanketed with police. It was eight o'clock, and the interview with Peter Galbraith had concluded. Standing in a side room with Tony Signorotto and Bryce Jones, Galbraith spoke.

"Do you think that interview might flush him out?"

Bryce Jones looked from Signorotto to Galbraith before speaking.

"If he watched that interview, Ziegler would be left in no doubt that you believe DVA and yourself are doing an incredible job looking after our returned troops. He would have seen red, though, when you answered the reporter and said that the person who attempted to kill you was a coward and lacked the guts to see you face to face. Let's see where this takes us from here," Jones said.

"There's been no sighting of him at your house or any trace of him around the outside of Channel Twelve. I think we had better get you back to the Melbourne Club and see what happens tomorrow. The boys who brought you here will take you back, and there will be a new crew inside the Club tonight for your safety," Signorotto said.

"Can't do more than bait the trap, I suppose," Galbraith said with a shrug of his shoulders. "But before we leave, I'd like to talk to that girl who interviewed me and have a chat about some initiatives that the Department of Veterans' Affairs is about to launch. Give me thirty minutes, if you would."

The two police officers had no choice in the matter, so they waited outside the reporter's office while she and Galbraith spoke.

***

Jack Ziegler had listened to Peter Galbraith's interview while he crouched down in the security guard's office. When it had finished, he raised his head to look outside and see if there was anyone around—which there wasn't.

With barely concealed rage, he picked up the small TV and slammed it into the concrete floor, smashing the screen into hundreds of tiny pieces. He then kicked the remainder of the instrument across the floor into a chair. Before turning the door handle and exiting, he spoke slowly to no one in particular.

"I am going to shove a gun down your throat while you are asleep and blow your fucking brains out, Galbraith. Call me a coward, will you? I'll take a video of you shitting yourself just before I pull the trigger and put it onto the Dark Web, and then the whole world can see you shake and cry before you die, you fucking hero," Ziegler said under his breath.

Putting both handguns into the back of his waistband, Ziegler ran quickly out into Little Collins Street and into Club Lane, where there was a large waste bin positioned next to the wall of the club. He jumped up onto the top and then leapt over the fence and onto the lower branches of the smaller of the palm trees. After swaying for a few seconds, he dropped quietly onto the ground and hid behind the trunk for about twenty seconds before making a dash for the back door. Looking carefully through a back kitchen window, he could see there was very little activity. For a week night, there was only one chef on, and he was sitting flicking through his iPhone.

He knew he wasn't dressed for the club, so he reached through the open kitchen door and removed a large white apron from a hook and put it on before turning around and picking up a box of apples from the ground and then disappearing back out into the yard, stepping into the back door as large as life. Next would be the tricky part: getting past the dining room and towards the entrance.

He only managed to get about ten steps inside before he was challenged.

"Where are you going with that?" questioned a tall, suited man wearing a gold name tag which displayed the name Greg and the words *Duty Manager*.

"Just taking them out to the van. Apparently, we've over-delivered. These are going up to the *Naval and Military Club*."

"The *Naval and Military Club* has been closed for two years. I should know because I was the manager there," the man said with a slow, suspicious-sounding voice.

With a quick look around, Ziegler could see that they were the only two people around. He slowly put the box of apples on a side table and quickly whipped one pistol out from the rear of his pants, pointing it directly at the manager's head.

"I presume you have a house phone you carry for when you walk around," Ziegler said quietly whilst pressing the firearm between the manager's eyes.

The man nodded in the affirmative as he slowly pulled the phone from his suit pocket. Sweat started to bead on his forehead, and his face turned an ashen colour.

"Good. Now I'm going to lower this gun, but rest assured it will only be inches from your back and ready to punch a hole right through your spine if you don't do exactly as I say. One slip-up, one wrong move of your head, and you will either be dead or a paraplegic. Do you understand?"

Again, the only thing the manager could do was nod slowly.

"You have another assistant on the front counter for when guests arrive?"

The nodding continued.

"Good. Now step into the next vacant room and get ready to make a phone call. What is the name of your desk man?"

"Anthony," the manager said with a quivering voice as they stepped into a small annex room.

Ziegler jammed the pistol into the small of the manager's back, forcing the man to give a grunt of pain. "Call Anthony and tell him you are just doing a quick check on the rooms before Peter Galbraith returns. What floor and room number is he on?"

"I can't tell you," were the only words that came out of his mouth before the butt of the pistol cracked into the back of his skull, knocking him to the ground. The hit wasn't a hard one, and

Ziegler dragged him back up by his arm and spoke again.

"One more time. My trigger finger is very twitchy at the moment. Next time, it may be far worse than a sore head," he said as the man held the back of his head while a trickle of blood seeped down over his fingers.

"Second floor, Room 201," the manager said with a now-terrified voice.

"That's better," Ziegler said, indicating with the pistol to make the internal call. The nervous finger of the manager pressed two buttons on the phone, which was quickly answered.

"Anthony, I'm just doing the rounds. Please be there when Mr Galbraith comes in. Thank you," he said before hanging up quickly.

"Good boy. Now let's head up to his room, shall we?" Ziegler said, nudging the manager towards the elevator.

The man staggered a few steps before pressing the elevator button. When they were inside, he pressed the button for the second floor.

***

The manager's assistant stared at the phone receiver. He had only worked at the Club a few months and was learning as much as he could. What made the phone call truly strange was that he knew that if a person of the standing of Peter Galbraith returned to the Club, it was an absolute matter of protocol that he be met by the manager, not some underling. The other thing that put him off-kilter was Galbraith telling him that he was 'doing the rounds.' That was never the job of the club manager. That was a job for the assistant. The manager never left the ground floor or the reception area. This was the place to greet all guests, and especially for members who suddenly decided they wanted to stay at the Club for the night without any reservation. This happened on a number of occasions with members of parliament, right up to the Prime Minister.

As he was slowly putting down the phone, one of the waiters walked past him with a smile on his face. "Do as I say, not as I do, eh, Anthony?" he said, tipping his head towards the elevator he had just passed.

"What are you talking about?" Anthony said.

"No staff to use the elevator at any time in case you end up side by side with the high and mighty. Bloody manager just got in and went to the second floor with some guy who looked like a derelict."

Anthony turned to see Peter Galbraith entering the front door along with two plain-clothes police officers. He knew about the guard that Galbraith had been given. Just as the Federal Government Head of Veterans' Affairs walked past him, the young assistant's voice called out.

"Please stop, sir. Something's wrong."

One of the members immediately grabbed Galbraith by the arm and pulled him back, while the other member swept his now-drawn firearm across the foyer at the same time as calling for back-up over his covert radio.

Galbraith was literally shoved back outside and into his car. It took off with a squeal of tyres east along Collins Street.

It seemed only seconds passed before the foyer was swarming with armed-to-the-teeth, black-clad Special Operations members.

Chapter 62

Tony Signorotto and Bryce Jones were shown through the outside perimeter of police tape that had been set up around the Melbourne Club by two uniform members from Melbourne East Police Station. They met with the Incident Commander, Inspector in the foyer.

"What I can tell you is this, guys," he said. "I've already spoken to the Assistant Manager, Anthony, and to one of the waiting staff who saw the Duty Manager, Greg Dutton, getting into the lift approximately thirty minutes ago with a scruffy-looking guy who matches the general description of your murder suspect, Jack Ziegler. Dutton had made an internal call to tell Anthony that he was going to check on the floors, which, according to Anthony, is only something an assistant does. Also, any staff using the lifts, including the General Manager, is a big no-no in case a VIP is in the lift. The building is only two floors and heavily carpeted, so by not using the lift all the time, noise is kept to a minimum. I would say our boy was going to ambush Galbraith when he walked into his room after the Channel Twelve interview. Thank Christ young Anthony was on the ball and jumped on our guys when they brought Galbraith in."

"So, what we're saying is that Ziegler is in Galbraith's room, holding Dutton as a hostage, and waiting for the door to open?" Jones said.

"I'd lay money on the fact that, within thirty minutes or so, when Galbraith hasn't opened the door, we will have a bigger siege situation on our hands than we do now. His room, 201, has a window that looks partially into the backyard so I've got that covered from the rooftop. If Ziegler looks out, he'll only see the top of a palm tree and a bit of the empty backyard. First things first, though—we have to get the other six occupied rooms evacuated. There's only two others on the second floor, with four on the first floor. How about we do that now, then make a phone call to Room 201?" the Inspector said.

"Good idea," Signorotto said to the Inspector, who immediately called four of his members over to brief them.

"I'll send two of them to keep an eye on the second-floor stairs, and the others can go with Anthony and quietly knock on the occupied rooms and get the members out," the Inspector said.

Fifteen minutes later, six weary-looking but compliant Melbourne Club members, together with five staff, were ushered into the foyer, then onto a police minibus in Collins Street.

***

Jack Ziegler knew something had gone wrong when, after almost forty minutes of waiting, there had been no sign of his quarry, Peter Galbraith. Even more conspicuously, there had been no call to the Duty Manager to inquire about his whereabouts. He had to get out of here. But how?

Greg Dutton had been sitting upright in a chair, virtually without moving, for all this time, and he could see Ziegler was getting very anxious. He took a punt and spoke.

"I can guarantee that police will be surrounding this building right now. As well as Peter Galbraith, you have some of the biggest captains of industry, and even the State Premier of Western Australia, in residence right now. Do you want me to ring reception and find out the situation?"

"Put it on loudspeaker," a sweating Ziegler said. Dutton pressed the number for reception. It was picked up immediately.

"Greg Dutton here. Who am I speaking to?"

"Inspector Worth from the Special Operations Group. First off, are you all right?"

"Yes, I am fine. I'm here in Room 2…"

Ziegler whipped the phone from his hand and switched it off. He had found out what he wanted to know—and that he really did have his back to the wall. He was in a room and surrounded by specialist police. As he leant back and stared at the ceiling, an idea dawned on him. In one corner of the ceiling was a manhole cover. He ran over to the heavy, old-fashioned drapes that were on the window and ripped four curtain tiebacks from both sides.

"Get on the floor, face down," he yelled at Dutton, who complied immediately, upon which Ziegler bound both his hands behind him, then tied his ankles together, after which he joined one of the ties from the ankle restraint to Dutton's tied wrists. He then went into the bathroom and came back with a monogrammed Melbourne Club face washer, which he stuffed into the Duty Manager's mouth. Dragging Dutton into the bathroom, he leant down and spoke quietly into his ear.

"For your sake, just stay there till they kick the door in. I am getting out of here, but if you make one sound while I get ready, I will happily put a gun to your head and pull the trigger. Understand?" Dutton nodded his head furiously, then put his face on the cool, tiled floor and shut his eyes.

Ziegler dragged the bed to a position under the manhole and then pulled the small antique writing desk over and placed it end-up on the bed. The building was old, and the ceilings were quite high, but it had to work. With his two pistols in his waistband, he carefully climbed onto the bed and then managed to balance on the upended desk. He stood very still until he had his balance. Carefully reaching up, he found he could easily push the manhole cover up and slide it to one side. This done, he reached up, grabbed one side of the square space above him, and with a grunt, pulled himself up into the roof space. If he had any chance of getting away with this, the only way was to find the inside part of the chimney and try to get onto the roof by removing tiles behind it and out of sight of any possible police on the roof next door. He was quite sure that there would be no police crawling around on the actual Melbourne Club roof, as it was a heritage-rated building, and all the tiles were made of slate—easy to remove from inside but also very fragile if you stepped on them.

Stepping from one internal roof beam to another, he made his way to where he believed the internal chimney was—the main one leading down into the old-fashioned dining room. He could smell the burnt wood before he eventually found the chimney. Not all the chimney bricks were even, so he managed to get a few footholds on and inched his way up to the slate roof. He paused before pulling a dozen or so slates back into the roof space and dropping them as quietly as he could onto the insulation batts. As he removed enough to crawl through, he could see some stars and feel a cool breeze over his face. He dragged himself through and sat gingerly on the exterior roof. Hidden by the chimney, he took in his position and realised that the roof of the building next door wasn't far from the wall of the Club.

Ziegler had pushed his luck, but he knew, to get away, he had to push it further. He decided to rest for a few minutes.

Resting was where his luck started to run out.

Chapter 63

The solid wooden door of Room 201 shattered like it was made out of matchsticks when it was struck by the metal hand-held battering ram known affectionately as 'the key'. Once it flew open, the large Special Operations Group member that wielded it stood to one side to allow his fellow officers to swarm into the bedroom.

Over the top of the shout of 'clear' which pertained to the room they had entered, the next voice shouted in reference to the hostage, Greg Dutton being safe and alive. Once these facts had been established, the SOG controller who was keeping the bedroom door clear, waved Bryce Jones and Tony Signorotto into crowded space. Several sets of eyes were peering at the open manhole while one member was hoisted up into the roof space.

No-one sat on formalities with Dutton. As the Duty Manager was having his hands and ankles untied, Signorotto quickly pulled the gag from the distressed man's mouth and even as he gulped in some breaths, Jones shoved a picture of Ziegler in front of him.

"Is this the man that has been holding you hostage tonight?" he said quickly.

A shaking Dutton nodded his head vigorously in the affirmative. "Yes, that's him, that's him. He threatened to kill me if I tried to make a sound after he tied me up. Said he'd happily pull the trigger if I as much as whispered."

As two more SOG members clambered up into the crawl space of the roof, Jones kept asking Dutton questions.

"Did he say anything about what he was going to do. Anything at all?"

"No, but he must have wanted to find Mr Galbraith because he only made me open this door, no others."

"Did you see how many guns he had?"

"Two. One on me and I saw another pistol in the back of his

trousers. He can't be more than five minutes in front of your guys up there. It took him a few minutes to get up, not like your fellows." Dutton said as Signorotto indicated to some SOG members to take the Duty Manager down stairs to a waiting ambulance.

"I have one guy scanning the roof from another building and I have four in the roof as well as two in the back yard," the SOG Commander said.

"I'm going out the front. That's the only place he can go without being seen. There are some uniform guys out there, but if Ziegler drops down on them they'll need back up," Signorotto said as he got up and ran for the door.

*****

Ziegler had taken a couple of minutes rest but when he heard a commotion underneath him coming from the roof crawl space he stood and made his way carefully to the roof area at the front of the building facing Collins Street. Looking down he knew it was impossible to get to ground level without injuring himself. He quickly turned to his left and could see the large old oak tree that had grown for probably a hundred years beside the Club. There was no other choice. Stepping up on to the flat concrete ledge that was part of the façade of the building he sprinted towards the tree just as a SOG member appeared in the periphery of his sight. He heard the words 'police stop' being yelled, but that just made him run faster.

Leaping from the concrete ledge, he felt like a cat burglar trying to roof hop as his arms windmilled through the empty space before he grabbed hold of a tree limb and swung down to the trunk where he crashed left shoulder first causing him to cry out in pain as his vision became stars before his eyes. He lost his grip and fell onto the top of two small garbage bins in the property next door.

Standing slowly he reached with his right hand to see if he still had his handguns. His left arm was totally numb. Trying to flex his fingers on his left arm he screamed in agony as he realised he had obviously broken the arm up near his shoulder. Somehow he managed to clamber over the side fence and staggered out into Collins Street about fifty metres from the front door of the Melbourne Club. Holding a pistol in his right hand he heard a shout from a fair way back.

"Stop Ziegler. Stop right there," Tony Signorotto yelled as he withdrew his service pistol and aimed it at the injured felon.

Ziegler ran into the roadway and pointed his firearm directly at the windscreen of a vehicle going the other way. As it skidded to a stop, he ran to the driver's door, yanking it open.

Tony Signorotto could do nothing. If he shot at Ziegler he could easily hit the terrified young woman who Ziegler was brandishing the gun at. All he could do was watch the girl fall onto the roadway. Ziegler jumped into the large four-wheel drive vehicle and while holding onto his pistol he started to drive away quickly while firing blindly back at Signorotto.

A scream erupted from the female on the road as Ziegler ran over one of her legs with the rear wheels. An incensed Signorotto aimed his pistol at the large moving target and fired four rounds into the side of the disappearing car. Ziegler's shots had all gone wide.

One SOG member appeared next to him and raised his shotgun to his shoulder in readiness to shoot before Signorotto put out his left hand and pulled the gun down. "Too late. Too dangerous now."

Bryce Jones came running across the road. "Did you hit him?" He said in an exasperated tone.

"Don't know," Signorotto said. "I certainly got the driver's door with a couple."

A round that had entered Ziegler's right leg above his knee proved Signorotto correct.

Chapter 64

The call had gone out immediately to bring in police cars from the surrounding areas. The whole of the CBD was being crisscrossed with patrols. The description of Ziegler and the stolen four-wheel drive was uppermost in the minds of all those searching for him.

Tony Signorotto, together with Bryce Jones, the SOG Commander, and Max Tyler were standing in the foyer of the Melbourne East police station. Signorotto was pacing up and down, cursing loudly.

"This bastard is making us look stupid. Before tonight, we could have picked him up, albeit without enough evidence for all his crimes. Now he is the outstanding, most sought-after crook this state has seen for years. He might not have got his prey tonight in regard to Peter Galbraith, but he has put another person in hospital. We have the owner of the car with a crushed leg, the kid who he shot up the other day, and a list of his crimes a mile long. We have to find him now," a clearly frustrated Signorotto said. "The papers will be all over tonight's fuck-up, and the Department will be crucified."

It had been two hours since Ziegler had taken off in the stolen car, and it had not been located.

"I know I have already asked you once, Tony, but do you think you may have hit him," Bryce Jones said quietly.

"I know I hit the driver's door with at least a couple right in the middle. He did swerve after the shots, so there's a chance that I may have put one in him. I just don't ...." Signorotto said, just as a junior member came running into the office where they were talking.

"The car's been found. It's in the car park of the Carlton footy club," the breathless constable said.

"Any sign of Ziegler?" the SOG Commander said as he reached for his portable radio.

"No, but there's a lot of blood, apparently, on the driver's side and the floor near the pedals, along with the inside of the door. The motor was still running. Parked half on the grass and the bitumen, and it looks like he ran into a steel pole there. Carlton 265 is up there now."

"That's Kate McLaren. She won't have a driver, so get onto D24 and get cars up there, but tell them to preserve the scene. We're on our way there," Signorotto said, leading the other two out of the door.

"I'll get a crew up there now," the SOG Commander said as he turned to speak into his radio, while Signorotto, Tyler, and Jones ran out.

As Tony Signorotto's mind started to clear, his focus went immediately to a good thing. He was heading back into Carlton territory, where he knew every little laneway, alleyway, and cul-de-sac. Ziegler had obviously been hit by one of his rounds, and that would slow the Sky Pilot down considerably, if not completely. As he drove flat out with Max Tyler beside him, he secretly hoped that Jack Ziegler would not be found dead in the park somewhere. The feeling in the back of his mind was that there was going to be a showdown. Not between Ziegler and Victoria Police, but between Ziegler and him.

Chapter 65

Jack Ziegler knew he was out of options. All his plans and schemes to wreak havoc on the warmongers that sent troops to fight battles that had nothing to do with Australia were now in tatters.

He had managed to wrap a towel that he had found in the hijacked car around his badly bleeding right leg, then limped and staggered from the car park across to the nearest grass area outside the wall of the football club. He then doubled back through the park and out into Royal Parade. He started to head toward the city, but looked down and could see the towel that was around his leg was becoming more saturated with blood every step he took. As he began to feel weaker, he crossed Royal Parade towards Royal Park, where he knew he could lay down out of sight and re-evaluate what he could do.

He had none of his drugs to support him, and his mind was becoming more clouded as he staggered along. Feeling behind his back, he took comfort in the fact that he still had his two pistols, and although he knew that he had let off some shots back in the city, he still had plenty left. He was not going to go down without a fight, and if he could take someone in authority with him, all the better. Just as he got near the intersection of The Avenue and Royal Parade, his leg went from under him, and he fell against a stone wall. It was then that he heard the ominous sound of police sirens and saw the red and blue colours in the distance toward the city. He tried to stand but couldn't. Suddenly it was all clear in his mind, and he sat upright against the cold wall and took out both of his pistols.

***

The car park of the Carlton Football Club was awash with red and blue flashing lights as members spilled out of their vehicles. Kate McLaren put out her hand to keep them away from the stolen four-wheel drive.

"Just keep back, guys. The Homicide Squad will be here in a minute, and this is a crime scene. Ziegler won't have gone far, so just spread out and get ready for some orders from Senior Sergeant Signorotto and the Special Operations Group."

Minutes later, Bryce Jones and Tony Signorotto drove in and went over to the car. When they looked at the ground, they could see droplets of blood leading out into the parkland.

"The SOG members will spread out and begin a slow search through the grass area toward the cemetery," the SOG Inspector called out. His troops were on the hunt within seconds, with him in the lead.

Bryce Jones was busy examining the inside of the hijacked vehicle along with Kate McLaren, as Tony and Max Tyler stood to one side. Tony started to walk up and down the car park in a nervous fashion, and just as he turned around at the edge of the car park, he spotted more blood drops on the kerb. Looking down, he could clearly see a trail of drops heading out to Royal Parade. He quietly signalled for Tyler to come over to him.

"Max, I think this bastard has double-backed. He's gone way into the park, hoping that the blood he is dropping will get lost amongst the trees and bushes. Let's you and I go this way," he said, heading off across the road before Tyler could virtually speak.

Max caught up with Signorotto on the other side of Royal Parade.

"Boss, be careful. Let's wait for back up," a worried Tyler said. Signorotto stopped and turned around.

"Max, I have made my mind up about the job. I'm finished after this. I've had enough, but I am not going to let this Ziegler prick get away with what he has done. Shooting and killing people in Carlton is something I will deal with, forgetting what else he has done in regard to murders and kidnapping. The guy is mad, and I want him badly before anything else happens. Then it's my time, Max. Mine and Susie's and Grace's."

"That's a dangerous way to search for someone, Tony. You sound as if this is some sort of showdown," Tyler said, facing the uniformed member. "Just bec…"

The sound and movement caught Signoretto off guard, but he still managed to grab hold of the detective just after the bullet had exited his suit jacket near the shoulder. Both members hit the ground, with Tyler screaming in pain. Signorotto grabbed Tyler by the legs and dragged him behind a tree.

"It's just you and him now, mate," Tyler said with a hoarse whisper as he grabbed hold of his old friend by the sleeve. Slowly letting go, he slumped his head on the ground as he closed his eyes. Blood pooled from his back. Signorotto could do nothing but stare down at the young detective. He was now beyond rage. Reaching under Tyler's jacket, he removed his pistol and kept it in his left hand. Looking around the tree, he saw the flash from the barrel of Ziegler's pistol some thirty metres away. He drew his own pistol from his holster and bolted to another tree closer to the shooter.

"If you want to live, Ziegler, then put down both pistols. Throw them out where I can see them," he shouted. The answer came back via several shots fired both near and far from Signorotto.

Tony knew exactly where Ziegler was. He could see him sitting against the stone. There were no other people anywhere near Ziegler, so Tony took aim and fired one shot. He knew he had hit him because one of the firearms flew from his hand and landed to one side. Tony sprinted towards the semi-incapacitated Ziegler. Taking aim again, Tony gave him one last chance as he came within metres of the smiling maniac.

"Drop the gun, Ziegler, or I will kill you where you are sitting."

Ziegler smiled and swung his pistol in an arc and started firing.

Tony Signorotto let one more shot go, hitting Ziegler dead centre and killing him.

Ziegler's body slid slowly sideways, causing a blood smear to appear across the Boer War memorial that he had unknowingly been sitting up against.

A fitting background for you, Tony thought as he lowered his weapons and fell to his knees. Looking at both the firearms, he began to sob, dropping them onto the ground.

The SOG Inspector, together with Bryce Jones and other members, converged on the shooting scene. Jones grabbed Signorotto by the shoulders and the Senior Sergeant slumped against him.

"Max, Max," Signorotto cried out as he looked back down the path to see a crying Kate McLaren rocking back and forth whilst holding the limp form of Detective Sergeant Max Tyler.

Chapter 66

The wedding of Chloe Schaeffer and Max Tyler had been planned for a long time before the terrible disaster had struck. There were going to be so many friends and colleagues, but time had moved on, and those plans had to be changed. *Such is life,* the saying went, but the two police officers had together overcome obstacle after obstacle and operation after operation. This time, nothing would stop them.

As Chloe looked down at her wheelchair-bound husband-to-be, a tear began to roll down her cheek before the hand of Tony Signorotto reached across with a handkerchief, which she took and dabbed it away with.

Max Tyler had undergone three surgeries to repair the damage the nine-millimetre round from Jack Ziegler's pistol had caused to his lungs and spine. The long-term prognosis was good, however. He had been in a wheelchair for the past three months but was now spending more time in the gym and was able to walk for twenty minutes at a time under supervision on the treadmill. His determination to stand for their wedding ceremony drove him on every day.

St. Carthage's church in Royal Parade, Carlton, was a happy place today. The pews were crowded with smiling faces of friends and workmates of both the bride and groom. Chloe's father, a former Assistant Commissioner, had died suddenly some months before, and Tony Signorotto was a proud man to be stepping in to give the lovely bride away.

On one side, Chloe had him as a proxy father, and on the other side, she had chosen Kate McLaren to be her maid of honour. She turned to Max and put out a hand as he rose from his wheelchair, which was quickly whisked away by one of his groomsmen. The entire congregation rose and clapped as Max slowly turned around and pumped one fist in the air—an action that made Tony Signorotto choke back tears.

As the ceremony commenced, Dom Santino could only think of

the reception that was planned for later that night at his restaurant *'Dom's'* in Lygon Street. It had never been an issue of where the festivities would take place; the only variable had been when, but even if his famous restaurant had been booked for that night, he would have cancelled all reservations for this great occasion.

There were friends and there was family, but to Dom and his wife Maria, the police from Carlton had always been both. It had been that way ever since a very young Tony Signorotto had befriended him one day when Dom had been a dishwasher at the restaurant, which he had later, after long hours and back-breaking work, bought and renamed. It had subsequently become a Carlton institution. He and Tony had both come from hard-working migrant backgrounds and were brought up on old traditions such as 'family first.'

The drama of Max's shooting at the hand of Jack Ziegler some months before was being put behind them, and they were looking forward to celebrating their special day with people such as retired Superintendent Phil Stone and one of the legends of the station, now long-retired former leading Senior Constable Jill Norton. It was going to be a night to remember.

***

Speech after speech had been given by many and varied people. With everyone, the rousing cheers had become louder and louder. Suddenly, though, the night was turned on its head by Tony Signorotto getting up on a table and asking for quiet.

Silence descended very quickly on the dance floor because there were a lot of members and even some ex-members who knew deep down what the legend who was Tony Signorotto was going to announce.

"Okay. We are all here tonight to celebrate Chloe and Max's wedding, which we have all been extremely grateful to attend. At the time, we didn't know if Max was going to pull through, but I can tell you that without your support, and especially Chloe's love for Max, it could have been a very different outcome. We wish them all the luck and love in the world going forward, and knowing Max as I do, it won't be long before he is out of that set of wheels permanently and back doing what he loves best, which is continuing to be one of the best police officers I have ever had the privilege to work with." A huge cheer echoed around the restaurant.

"As to the brilliant reception that Dom and Maria Santino have put on, well, we didn't really expect anything less, did we? As long as I've been at Carlton, and that is now a very long time, the Santino family has looked after our family of blue here in Lygon Street for everything that could be covered by the Births, Deaths, and Marriages Registry." Another huge roar went up.

"Now, I know that some of you want to know what's going on with me. The good old police rumour mill has been in overdrive, I hear, and just because I have taken the last month off on sick leave doesn't mean I don't love you all. I have been genuinely tired and not up to the rigours of being your officer-in-charge. I probably came back too soon from my own injuries, but I can assure you I am okay, and Max and I are having a show and tell with bullet wounds later in the night for only twenty dollars a peep."

With this comment, the crowd roared with laughter, and a couple of the younger brigade of members came rushing forward with their credit cards, wanting to book a showing.

"Sorry, guys, but it's strictly cash only, due to us not wanting any paper trail going back to Internal Affairs," Tony said, laughing before continuing.

"Getting back to what I need to tell you is that I have decided to take long service leave for the next three months, and if I do come back, it will most likely not be to a station as a Senior Sergeant. Folks, the motor is a bit old now, and it's like my old GT Ford Falcon that I drive, in that it will be brought out only if needed for special occasions. My beautiful and long-suffering wife and I, together with little Grace, our daughter, are going on a pilgrimage back to Italy, along with Dom and Maria Santino. We both have a lot of family we haven't seen for years. It is a trip without a timeline for all of us. I think I have had enough of spending day after day in blue so I can tell you this. I have told the big bosses of my plan and they have decided, with my blessing, to appoint Kate McLaren as the new Officer-In-Charge of Carlton as of next week. She was told about this a few days ago so now she can let the cat out of the bag."

Kate McLaren waved from the back of the room as members came up to congratulate her.

One of the long serving Carlton Senior Constables called from a table.

"Who's going to be the new number two Senior Sergeant?"

"Well, I won't keep you in suspense any longer, but from next week, and starting on a restricted comeback to station work only, is the newly, from today, Second in Charge of the Carlton Police Station, the one and only Senior Sergeant Max Tyler," Tony said sweeping his arm down to a totally gob-smacked Max who had no idea of his promotion. Chloe burst into tears beside him.

"I couldn't leave you in more capable hands than those of Kate and Max. I'm not saying I won't be back, who knows? Now enjoy the rest of the night," an almost tearful Tony Signorotto said as he climbed down from the table into the arms of his wife Susie... and about twenty of the members who came up to give the Legend of Carlton a hug.

Off to one side, Superintendent James Collins was sipping on a glass of Pinot Noir when a voice behind him spoke with a quiet but steady tone. It was that of Assistant Commissioner Vic Merchant from Headquarters.

"He'll be back. The Chief has plans for him. Big plans, but don't say anything to him, James. Let him have his time in Italy. Now speaking of plans, I need to see you next week in relation to a new Task Force which I want you to head up."

"What type of Task Force and when?"

"Tell you all about it next week. You'll be able to pick your members. One or two of them might be in this room right now. You'll have time to settle in. Don't want it up and running for about three months, which just happens to coincide with the return of a certain person over there," he said turning to look at the mobbed figure of Senior Sergeant Tony Signorotto.

Collins raised his glass of red to the Assistant Commissioner's smile.

"Cin Cin," he responded.

THE END

About the Author

Phil Copsey served with Victoria State Police Force, Australia, for forty years. His hard-earned experience fighting crime on the streets of multicultural Melbourne compelled him to write his true policing books, **Blue Justice**, **The Calibre of Justice**, **The Hand of Justice** and **Killing Justice**. His depictions of characters and crimes are infused with authentic operational details, told through the eyes of his composite character, Sergeant Tony Signorotto. Phil is a natural storyteller who returned to study towards the end of his career to begin his Tony Signorotto crime series.

*

You are welcome to email the author at
philipcopsey@gmail.com

By the same author

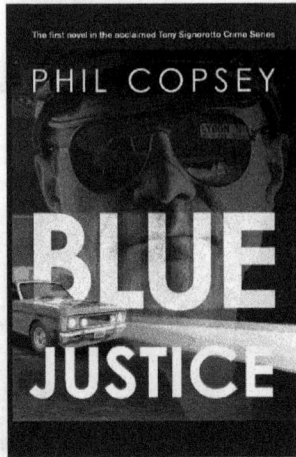

Blue Justice is the first of a gritty new crime series published by in case of emergency press.

Don't look for puzzling cases, corpses in locked rooms, ingenious criminal masterminds, this is a novel about police on the beat: ugly, raw, and morally uncertain. It's not about solving crime. It's about solving problems.

Sergeant Tony Signorotto has good friends, plenty of enemies, and the sort of family connections that just might get him killed.

Buy **Blue Justice** from
https://icoe.com.au/bluejustice.html

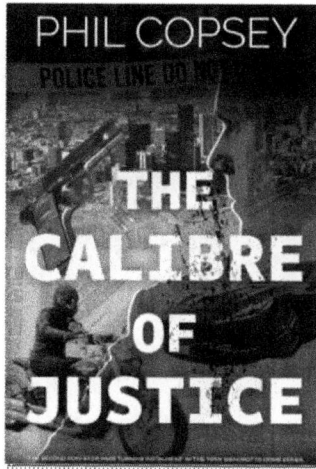

The Calibre of Justice continues the story of Tony Signorotto, now
newly promoted to the rank of Senior Sergeant, at his beloved Carlton
Police Station. Now married to his long-time girlfriend, Tony is looking
to extend his career and look after his charter of the safety of the suburb
of Carlton in Melbourne's north.

   Life should be less complicated. He has made the sacrifice of life on
the edge for nine-to-five and the paperwork routine surrounding his
mahogany foxhole—until the rumours of a possible firearms raid on the
Victoria Police Department. Enough handguns, if stolen, to flood the
streets of Carlton and every major city in Australia.

   Fast-paced, and brilliantly plotted, The Calibre of Justice is also
frighteningly real!

Buy **The Calibre of Justice** from
https://icoe.com.au/thecalibreofjustice.html

THE HAND OF JUSTICE

THE THIRD INSTALLMENT IN THE TONY SIGNORETTO CRIME SERIES

PHIL COPSEY

The Hand of Justice is an intriguing mix of politics, policing, and power. The stakes are high and reputations will be made or lost.

A new threat has emerged on the streets of Carlton, and it is one of their own in the blue uniform. Do they trust him to see if he can save himself and his career? Or do they give him just enough rope to hang himself?

This thrilling continuation of Phil Copsey's 'Justice' series will take them on a journey that spans illegal gambling, the Russian mafia, an international begging scam, and down a one-way path of murder and kidnapping.

Buy **The Hand of Justice** from
https://icoe.com.au/thehandofjustice.html

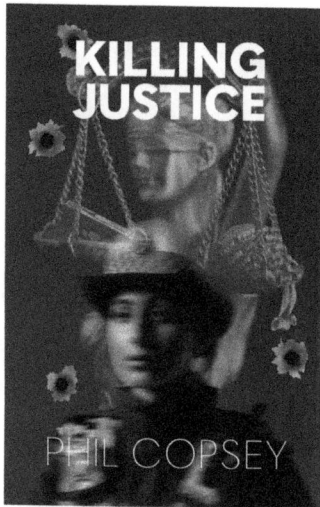

Bogdan Vulpe's empire is ruled with an iron fist. No one disobeys. That had been his way in Romania; so why should the City of Melbourne be any different?

Killing Justice leads you into a world of unbridled violence. Murder, extortion and anything else that Volpe needs to succeed will be used. If he has to take retribution against officers of the highest court in the land, so be it.

This latest challenge to Tony Signorotto and his loyal team is his toughest yet. Not only is he battling a violent criminal gang, but changes in the ranks of his beloved Carlton police force will pit him against an ambitious, careerist police Superintendent more interested in glory than justice. The fight to uphold the laws of the State continue in the gripping fourth instalment in the Tony Signorotto crime series.

Buy **Killing Justice** from
https://icoe.com.au/killingjustice.html

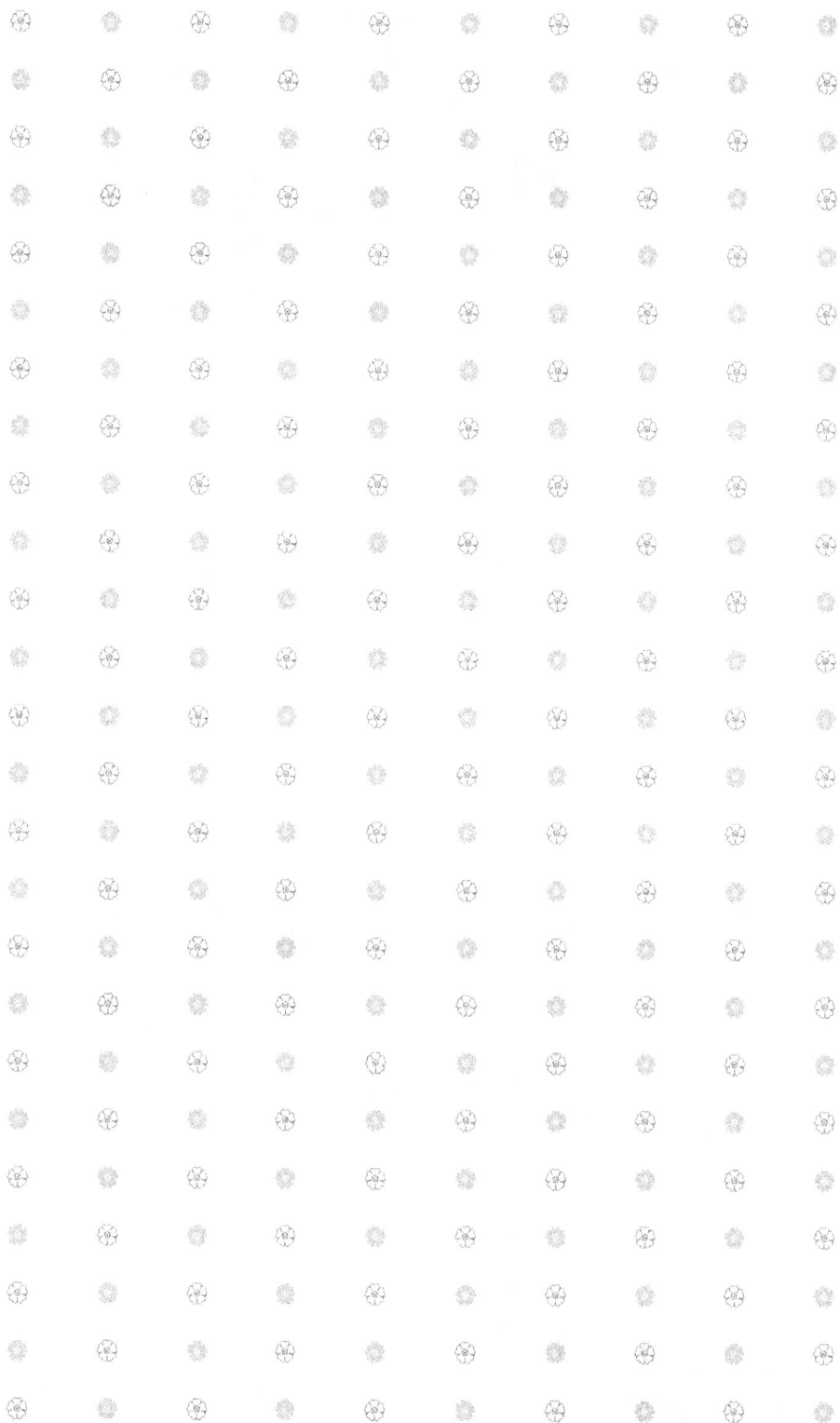

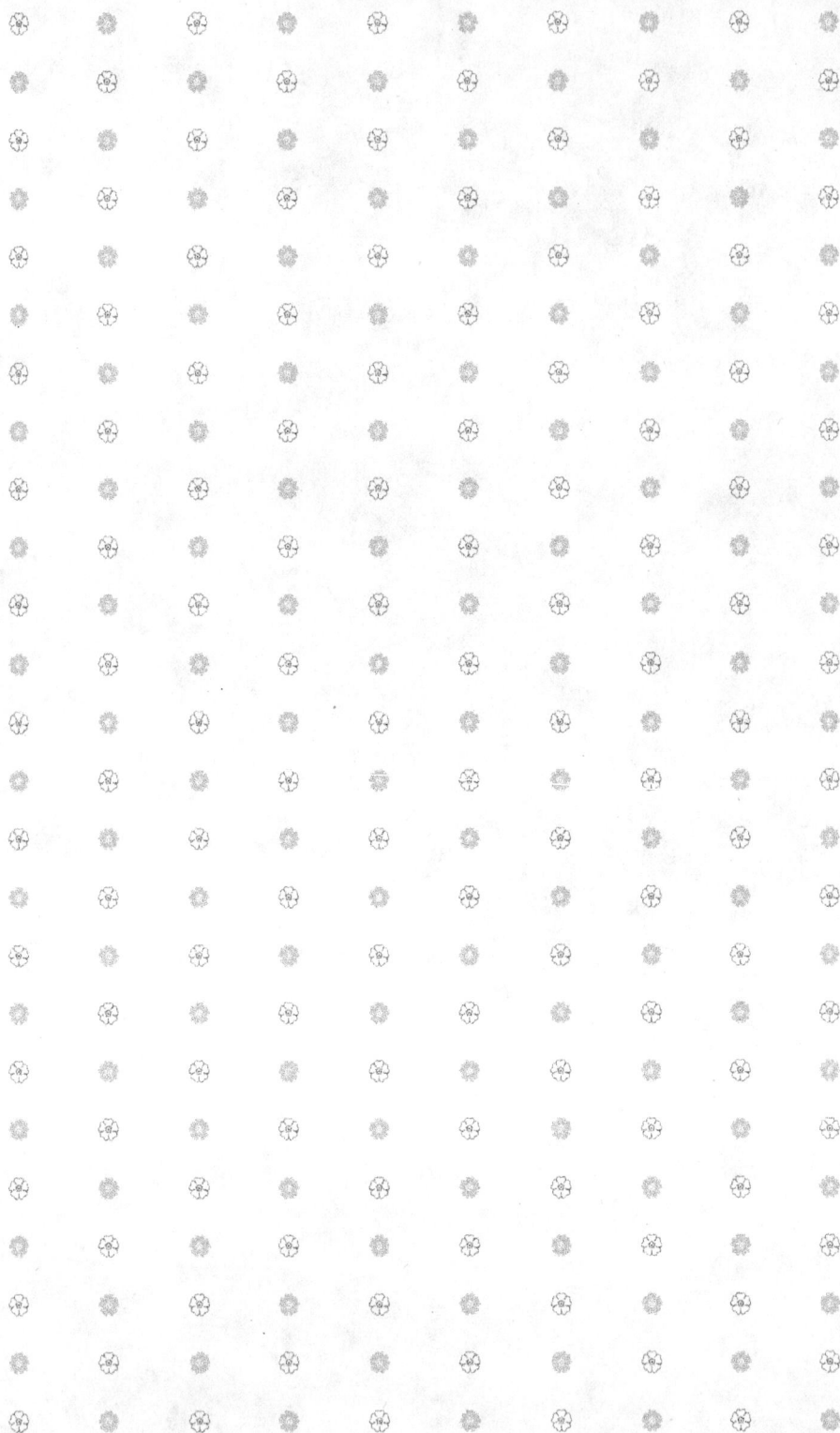